TRAINING YOUR OWN BIRD DOG

Training Your Own
BIRD DOG

∽∽∽∽∽∽∽∽∽∽∽∽∽∽∽∽∽∽∽∽

HENRY P. DAVIS

New Revised Edition

∽∽∽∽∽∽∽∽∽∽∽∽∽∽∽∽∽∽∽∽

G. P. PUTNAM'S SONS

NEW YORK

To MYRA,

    my wife, whose more than forty years of
uncomplaining labor as kennel-boy, patient
nurse, and puppy-mopper-upper-after will
surely win her a place in heaven,
this book is gratefully dedicated.

Henry P. Davis

BIRD DOG

Deep chest, slim flank, great heart to stand the pace,
And that unerring wizardry of scent
To trail the quarry in its secret place;
Power and cunning, speed and wisdom blent—
These are the immemorial gifts that came
Out of forgotten time's unfathomed gulf;
These are the fierce ancestral fires that flame
Undimmed, unchanging still—Son of the Wolf.

Grave eyes, grave bearing, dignity of kings;
The gentleness and trust as of a child;
The flawless poise that veils old savage things
But half-remembered from the vanished wild—
These are the knightly qualities that came
On unremembered fields where sports began;
This is the clear glow of a steady flame
Undimmed, unchanging still—Comrade of Man.

C. T. DAVIS

CONTENTS

ILLUSTRATIONS

(after page 84)

INTRODUCTION

IN PRESENTING that puppy to Tom, I was really conducting an experiment. For a long time I had been firmly convinced that the average man of even temper and moderate patience, given a fair knowledge of the general principles of training and good material to work with, could develop his young bird dog into a valuable and well-mannered shooting companion. And Tom was an average man.

A recent convert to the sport of hunting, he knew very little about dogs—and was aware of the fact. But he was a good listener, anxious to learn and willing to try to put sound theory into practice. He had no preconceived ideas or fantastic formulas. The puppy I gave him was of average precocity, well-bred, and physically sound. So the two of them started from scratch, as it were.

Now tune in on Tom two years later: "Look him over. He's a real bird dog now. Cocksure and confident. Practically finished and, thanks to some of your suggestions, most of his faults have been corrected. He understands me and I understand him. I can't tell you how much fun I'm having in training him."

My friend's buoyant enthusiasm was warranted. And in it lies, I feel, the justification for this book. There are thousands of Toms interested in training their own dogs but reluctant to take up the task, because they believe the principles involved are too technical for inexperienced hands. This book is written in the belief that this doubt, in some small measure at least, can be dispelled. If in these pages discouraged sportsmen find renewed confidence, the writer will feel that his work has not been in vain.

This book is directed particularly at the sportsman or sportswoman who has had no previous experience in educating field dogs, who is interested in the practical rather than the theoretical side of training, and who desires to secure the greatest amount of pleasure possible from working his own dog. Hence what follows will be rudimentary in its scope and, while it is hoped that much of interest to the initiated and the professional will be found herein, it is expressly designed to aid the beginner.

Let us, then, look upon bird-dog training as a recreational pastime and not as a vocation. Bird-dog training was a pastime long before it came to be recognized as an outright profession. In his *Art of Fowling*, written in 1621, Markham devoted a chapter to the "setting dogs," their type, colors, and training. Concerning training he wrote: ". . . In divers places in this kingdome these Setting-Dogges are to be taught (so that most men of ability may have them at their pleasures) yet likewise I know they are sould at such great rates and prizes that no industrious man whatsoever (which either loves the sport or would be partaker of the benefit) but will be glad to learne how to make such a dogge himselfe, and so both save his purse and make his pleasure and profit both more sure and more delicate." So even in those early days when the art of bird-dog training was in its infancy and its principles known to but a few, Markham believed that it offered recreational opportunities and that success in this sport was not beyond accomplishment by the average man.

The amount of pleasure to be derived from your bird dog reaches its maximum only when you have trained him yourself. It is then you will have seen him develop from a shamble-gaited puppy, wondering what the world holds in store for him, into a mature and finished shooting dog, completely cognizant of his purpose in life, who dashes afield with glad confidence he is fully equipped to enhance the day's pleasure for his master.

The constant glow of pleasurable satisfaction that accompanies the knowledge you have developed, trained, and finished your own shooting dog is well worth the time, effort, and often discouraging inconvenience that must be encountered in the task. And the fact that the task is not always an easy one makes the pleasure that accompanies its successful completion all the more enjoyable.

The value of a perfectly trained shooting dog can be fully appreciated only after one has attempted to secure a day of field pleasure behind a wild harum-scarum type of bird dog that has not had the advantages of good training. The ideal field combination is realized when the master has complete confidence in his dog, and the dog has complete confidence in his master. This most often results when the master has trained his own dog, for it is then that the dog has grown up, both in a physical and intellectual way, with his owner. Complete understanding on both sides is then evident. It is toward this end that this book is directed.

HENRY P. DAVIS

TRAINING YOUR OWN BIRD DOG

Chapter 1

MASTER AND PUPIL

⚛

THE DOG can learn much from his master, and an observant master can learn much from his dog. The dog is generally willing and anxious to learn, but unfortunately many masters are unwilling to devote the time and painstaking effort necessary in training methods to bring the dog to a full and complete realization of what the master wants him to do. Once the dog fully understands what his trainer is trying to teach him, the task is almost completed.

It does not remain that all dogs will develop under any methods into excellent performers in the field. There are some individuals that simply do not possess the natural qualities necessary for this accomplishment, and no matter how hard the trainer tries he cannot bring them to a degree of field excellence. Simply, the spark of spirit or heart is lacking. Such individuals should be discarded as worthless.

Neither does it hold that every man will make a successful bird-dog trainer. Some persons have a particular flair for educating or training animals. Some of these individuals have developed this quality through practical experience. In others it lies dormant because of lack of interest. But it is safe to say that any man who is sufficiently interested to try and who can exercise a fair degree of self-control can, through the careful application of the training principles outlined in this book, develop the average young pointer or setter into a good shooting dog.

It must be borne in mind that bird-dog training is not all "breaking" and that the teaching of certain things and the correction of certain faults are not the only parts of a dog's training.

Training is teaching the dog what he should do, and the most successful trainer will accomplish this in such a manner that the dog will respond to his desires willingly without the full realization that some of the actions demanded are against his natural instincts. Training is a combination, in the proper proportion, of curbing and encouraging the bird dog's natural inclinations and instincts.

Breaking might be well defined as the curbing of a dog's natural inclinations and the molding of his actions to suit one's will, generally against the natural desires of the dog.

Training is teaching; breaking is making. Well-broken is a common and rather loosely used term to describe a finished performer. It does not necessarily mean that the dog has been forced to behave properly, although the term implies that probability.

In training it often becomes necessary to resort to mild force to make the dog realize that he must do certain things and must not do certain other things. But to complete properly the pupil's education one must encourage certain natural qualities and develop to the highest degree possible those natural instincts that make a bird dog the greatest asset to his master's gun.

We know that under certain conditions most dogs will react to certain treatment in the same way. Thus we can use practically the same methods to cause most dogs to do certain things. However if we curb his natural inclinations too strenuously, we run the risk of destroying his self-confidence and independence and of making him into a mechanical dog entirely dependent upon his master for hunting instructions.

On the other hand, if we allow him an entirely free head and make no effort to turn his natural instincts into the proper channels, we again minimize his chances of becoming the proper aid to the gun.

While the dog must be possessed of certain qualities before he can become a candidate for shooting-dog honors, so must the man have certain attributes before he can qualify as a successful trainer.

There are three great P's in bird-dog training, which every successful handler must possess. They are Patience, Persistence, and Practical Knowledge of the job at hand: Patience (which includes that priceless quality, self-control) carefully and painstakingly to teach the necessary lessons even in the face of discouraging resistance on the part of the pupil day after day; Persistence in the application of proper training methods until the pupil is letter-perfect in his lessons; and Practical Knowledge of the job at hand in order to know when and how to act, and when and why not to act.

The first lesson the trainer himself must learn is that of self-control. The work of hours and even days of patient training can be wholly undone and the dog's confidence in his trainer entirely shattered in one foolish burst of temper. It is naturally exceedingly trying for the beginner to see his young pupil disregard all his apparently well-learned lessons on occasions, but experienced trainers know that such happenings are bound to occur and take them as a matter of course.

In fact, when the young pupil goes stale on his training, it is often best to allow him more latitude for a while.

Patience is the first virtue in dog training, and the failure of most spoiled dogs may be traced to the lack of this quality in the make-up of the trainer. Remember that a light hand. a soft voice, and a high heart are part of the equipment of a successful trainer.

And we must possess or develop persistence in a high degree. Persistence to try to teach the same lessons day in and day out, over and over again until they are thoroughly understood by the pupil. Persistence to correct errors without show of temper at the right time and in the right manner; and persistence in acknowledging by rewards of tidbits or caresses work well done.

A practical knowledge of the job in hand is most essential if the best results are to be obtained. First, the trainer should acquaint himself with the qualities that go to make up a high-grade, well-trained shooting dog. He should form an ideal in his own mind and then strive to have his pupil conform to that ideal. Tastes in bird dogs differ as they do in "shoes and ships and sealing wax" and the type of dog that pleases one individual may not be acceptable to another. However, these differences of opinion are generally of a minor nature, and the standards of bird-dog excellence are fairly well established. They are practically the same in all localities, whether it be in quail, pheasant, prairie-chicken, grouse, or woodcock country, the main differences being in the matter of range and the manner of working out a given section of country. It does not necessarily hold that a good quail dog ever will develop into a good grouse dog or that a dog trained in pheasant country will confine himself to woodcock covers successfully, but this is not an impossibility, and many examples of this adaptability have been noted.

It might be well to define here just what constitutes a

good shooting dog, in order that we may be thoroughly conversant with the ideal toward which we are to strive.

The first requisite of an excellent shooting dog is, to my mind, the ability to size up his country and work it intelligently. By working it intelligently I mean in such a manner as to take in all the birdy places without lost time and wasted effort and with the thought of his master and the gun always in his mind. Some dogs have this quality instinctively, but it generally comes with experience and is a faculty that the trainer can assist his pupil in acquiring.

Some dogs have better or more sensitive noses than others, but no shooting dog can completely fulfill his purpose unless he is possessed of a good nose. This is a physical quality that cannot be acquired by training, for a dog simply has or has not a good nose.

An excellent shooting dog properly adapts his pace and range to the country in which he is hunted. In open sections obviously barren of game, he wastes no time but speeds on to the likely spots and, whether his master be mounted or afoot, adapts his pace and range to suit the occasion.

Possessed of a good nose and the ability to apply his speed and range and hunting instincts intelligently, a good shooting dog must know how to handle game when he finds it. This ability is generally the product of the trainer's art, although there are dogs known as naturals or born broken. This is indeed the exception to the rule, and the owner should never depend on his pupil to break himself. The proper shooting dog must stop instantly when he finds game, assume a motionless or somewhat cataleptic posture, and remain thus stanch while his trainer comes to flush his birds. The perfectly trained shooting dog remains steady to shot and wing, i.e., he retains his motionless posture until ordered on by his trainer, although the birds have been flushed and the shot fired. Some sportsmen prefer to allow their dogs to break shot to retrieve, but such dogs cannot be called perfectly broken in the true sense of the term.

A pleasing shooting dog should have good style. This term style may be defined as the manner in which a bird dog does things. It is equally applicable to his carriage in the field and his attitude on point. It is a physical quality that is possessed or not possessed. The trainer can spoil a dog's style, but seldom can he improve it.

Often a young dog begins his field career with mediocre style, but improves in this quality as his self-confidence increases. An exceedingly timid dog or one that has been hacked, cramped, or too strenuously forced in his training seldom has good style, either in action or on point, and the trainer must be very careful not to hamper this most pleasing characteristic.

After all, the owner derives most pleasure from the quality of the work rather than the quantity, and a dog of pleasing action, which snaps into bold, intense postures on game, is indeed a beautiful thing to behold. While loftiness on point is a thing to be desired for several reasons, a much more important quality is the intensity of positiveness. When the two are combined the acme of perfection has been reached.

A dog that stands on his game in a lofty attitude but without the rigidity of intenseness cannot be rated as stylish. And the dog that continually looks around or moves about on his game can be faulted for sloppiness on point. The stylish dog is one that hunts in a dashing manner, with high head and merry tail, and that goes to his game boldly, establishing a positive and intense point.

Obedience is most essential in the shooting dog. He may have natural intelligence, a good nose, adaptability, perfect manners on game, and excellent style and even then may not be rated as a top shooting dog if he does not handle to his master's gun.

The well-trained dog hunts for his master and does not continually make his own course, thus forcing his master to hunt for him. I do not mean that a dog should depend entirely upon his master for instructions, for independence and initiative are essential in a good shooting dog. But he must respond to his master's commands immediately and willingly.

The dog that has been properly trained can be taught to obey commands immediately without the loss of any of his self-confidence or initiative. He must be brought to realize that his purpose in life is to serve his master to the best of his ability, and once this realization dawns on him he will generally try to fulfill his mission gladly.

The perfect shooting dog must instantly back or honor his bracemate's point on sight or at command. And lastly he must retrieve promptly and tenderly. Coming to heel, dropping to shot, dropping at command, stopping instantly at command, and remaining dropped until ordered on are niceties of training, desirable although not absolutely essential.

This may seem a rather large order for the beginner. It is, however, only an ideal to bear in mind, an ultimate goal to strive for, which can be reached only if you have the best material and exercise the proper care in training.

I have said that some men have more aptitude for dog training than others. This does not preclude the possibility of fair success in dog training by the average person who will carefully and studiously devote himself to the principles of the art. Perhaps we cannot all be outstanding bird-dog trainers, but we can, with the aid of the three great P's, direct the forces that govern the actions of fair bird-dog prospects and mold these youngsters into good hunting companions over which it will be a pleasure to shoot. The expectancy of success depends upon both individuals, human and canine. Know yourself and then know your dog. The next step will be to start his education.

All bird dogs are individuals. None are alike, and while the broad principles of bird-dog training are generally applicable to most pointers and setters, there are always exceptions to the rule. It is then that the ingenuity of the trainer is brought into play, and he must invent methods to fit the individual case.

It would be unfair to expect every bird-dog puppy to develop into a high-class shooting dog, just as it would be to expect every male child to become a master of industry. Breeding, environment, and education all play their parts toward the development of the youngster and must be recognized.

There are certain natural qualities that are easily recognizable in the good bird-dog prospect, but still there is no assurance that the most precocious puppies will develop into the best dogs at maturity. Some youngsters develop earlier than others; the pointing instinct is more latent in some individuals; the desire to hunt must be encouraged in some and controlled at an early age in others.

So it behooves the beginner to build a firm foundation of knowledge as to the requisites of a good bird dog, choose his prospect with care, and then carefully study the various characteristics of that individual.

Know yourself and know your dog. Then start his education.

Chapter 2

PRINCIPLES OF TRAINING

⚭

MOST BIRD DOGS can be taught easily to do certain things because their natural instincts lean toward the accomplishment of these certain things. Thus training in these instances becomes merely a matter of the development and direction of natural instincts. Other qualities of performance are against the natural inclinations of the dog and hence must be developed through the trainer's art or genius.

And so the principles of bird-dog training may be defined as those steps directing the development of the natural instincts that are useful, the curbing of the traits that tend to detract from the dog's field performance, and the teaching of these niceties of character and finish necessary in the make-up of the high-class shooting dog.

The first natural instinct of the well-bred dog is the inherent desire to hunt. In some individuals this quality asserts itself at an earlier age than in others. In some rare instances this quality never becomes apparent in any appreciable degree, and these individuals should be discarded as worthless.

The hunting instinct must be encouraged in the young dog, and it can seldom become overdeveloped. Yet at the same time it must be controlled and molded so that the method of hunting will meet the desires of the trainer and conform to the type of territory in which the dog is used. For instance, the long, sweeping casts of the quail or prairie-chicken dog would be of little service in ruffed-grouse country, and the quartering methods of the grouse dog would be out of place in open country obviously barren of game.

The ideal dog, in respect to the hunting instinct alone, is one that will adapt his range to the country before him and his method of hunting to the type of game bird to be found in that country.

The pointing instinct characteristic of bird dogs is naturally highly developed in some youngsters and more latent in others. In fact in some dogs the pointing instinct is so sluggish that careful and painstaking methods must be employed to teach them to point.

The action of pointing is not in reality a single, separate instinct but is the result of a combination of instincts that work together in such rapid harmony that the function appears to be the response to a single urge. The scent affects both nerves and muscles and brings them into play in such a manner that a definite point results.

Stanchness in point, in the degree necessary in the finished shooting dog, cannot be termed in itself a natural instinct but is the development of a quality that automatically accompanies the pointing instinct. Seldom do we find the dog that breaks himself, and in these rare instances the dog is not so dependable in stanchness as the one in which this quality has been developed through the trainer's genius.

Adaptability, or the quality that causes a dog to hunt out all types of cover intelligently and with proper range, comes naturally to some dogs, but most generally it is apparent only in dogs that have been often hunted in territories having a wide variety of cover types. It can be developed by the trainer, but it will be of comparatively little concern to the beginner in bird-dog training, for he is probably most interested in developing his own dog to suit his local requirements.

Self-hunting, flushing, and chasing are all natural instincts of the bird dog, which must be curbed and controlled. Any of these traits is often sufficient to tax the trainer's ability to the utmost, but for each of these faults there is a remedy, the proper application of which will bring about correction.

The problem with which the amateur trainer is confronted is the development of the young and inexperienced prospect into a finished field performer without causing him to lose any part of his boldness, dash, or independence. The finished field performer is one that utilizes his natural instincts and abilities to the best interests of his master and makes his own desires secondary to his master's commands.

Bird-dog training is a fascinating pastime and offers great possibilities in the matter of recreational pleasure. The beginner is often prone, however, to become so interested in the training of his young charge that he overdoes the job and as a result his prospect becomes a mechanical dog constantly looking to his master for instructions and wasting valuable time that should be spent in hunting. So it is necessary that the beginner achieve the correct mental attitude before he launches into his efforts as a teacher.

Many of us are of the opinion that bird-dog training is a rudimentary art wherein the strict adherence to a few set principles will accomplish the ultimate goal. A man may memorize every training method yet devised and be absolutely letter-perfect in the general principles, but if he does not know how, when, and why to apply these methods, he is doomed to failure.

The proper application of training principles requires an infinite amount of patience and self-control. No matter how readily the young prospect takes to his lessons and responds to his training, he is bound to break over someday and either do everything wrong or completely refuse to go through his paces. It is then that the self-control of the trainer is taxed to the utmost. Most of us resent the idea that we might be lacking in self-control. This resentment is plain vanity and must be overcome in bird-dog training, for canine pupils can at times be the most exasperating charges imaginable.

Bird dogs are individuals and not machines. Each one is different in many respects and offers different angles in the psychological element of bird-dog training. None is a jigsaw puzzle to be put together piece by piece, but each is possessed of different characteristics and different emotional tendencies that must be studiously observed by the trainer, who must build his training program around these physical and mental factors.

While the broad principles are generally applicable, each must be varied to fit the individual and exceeding care must be exercised to "get the right shoe on the right foot." A method that might cause a bold dog to do certain things might be a direct contribution to the ruination of a timid dog. You can place a sluggish, lethargic colt of one of the draft breeds in harness and break him to teamwork in short order by the use of force. But try that on a high-strung thoroughbred youngster and a spoiled horse results. So it is with a bird dog.

The trainer must *know* every characteristic of his dog and through this knowledge must sense just how far he can go with him in certain directions. And he must *never* venture beyond this danger line until the psychological moment arrives. This intuition is a very definite part of the trainer's art. It is acquired only through experience and studious observation and, regardless of experience, some people have more faculty for acquiring it than others.

The beginner must *know himself*. And knowing himself, he must carefully guard his actions to prevent even the slightest loss of self-control. Frankly, even then he cannot be expected to maintain an even mental keel constantly, for his patience will be sorely tried on many occasions. But his own efforts will be thwarted by any submission to an outburst of temper.

Young dogs are exceedingly susceptible to both mental and physical influences. An excited attitude is transmitted to the pupil much more rapidly than the average beginner realizes. The trainer who does not watch himself carefully is bound to become ruffled or excited on occasion. It is then that his manner of expression changes, his voice takes on a new inflection, and even his facial features reflect his mental unevenness. The dog almost immediately catches the spirit of this attitude and becomes excited or uneasy himself. When this condition occurs it is best that the trainer leave off teaching until another and more fortunate occasion, for no good work can be accomplished, and continued efforts under these circumstances will only result in confusion.

Knowing when to stop is a priceless attribute of the art of training. The trainer who can maintain a calm demeanor, even in the face of trying circumstances, is the one whose efforts will be attended by the most success, for an even, unruffled, confident manner on the part of the handler imparts confidence to the dog and is helpful in holding his undivided attention.

And without his undivided attention little can be accomplished. Never attempt to teach a lesson in surroundings that will not allow privacy or where disturbing elements may divert the dog's attention from the task you have set for him to perform. Many beginners become so enthusiastic over the progress of their pupils that they invite friends to look on during the teaching of a lesson. This generally results disastrously, for the attention of the dog is diverted, he fails to live up to the lavish statements of his fond owner, the audience is disappointed, and the trainer generally comes in for a share of good-natured panning, which, though intended in fun, is usually both embarrassing and discouraging.

Never allow a lesson to last too long. Fifteen minutes is generally long enough to spend at one time in yard-breaking lessons. The trainer should watch his dog carefully and try to maintain his interest. At the first sign of fatigue or lagging interest the lesson should be discontinued and a short romp or walk engaged in.

"All work and no play makes Jack a dull boy" is applicable to canine as well as human pupils, and the trainer who attempts to carry his lessons too far at any one time is merely working against himself, as the dog is more than apt to become sullen and stubborn.

Because a young dog is bold and takes to training readily is no reason why he should be crowded too fast. The constant rehearsing of one phase of yard breaking, such as retrieving, becomes irksome in time and the lesson should end when the dog is doing his best work. Care must be taken to keep the pupil on edge at all times. Repetition of lessons learned earlier in his training may serve to revive a lagging interest and break the monotony of the lesson for the day. Once the young dog has become tired or sullen, he should not be forced to continue, for herein lies the danger of breaking his spirit and both trainer and pupil must suffer.

The successful trainer will study his pupil carefully, learn as much as possible about his likes and dislikes, his various mental and physical characteristics, and then adopt a program designed to best suit the individual. His training methods will be directed toward teaching the various accomplishments in such a manner that the dog will be anxious to learn, the lessons taught will be well remembered, and the dog will have such complete confidence in his master that he will constantly strive to please. It is then that the ideal will have been realized—a master with full knowledge of his dog's good qualities and shortcomings, and perfect confidence in his abilities, and a dog that idolizes his master and strives to give him his best at all times.

The pleasure of shooting over such a dog that you have developed yourself is well worth the time and effort in training, for the man who is successful in this has himself learned many lessons in patience and self-control.

Chapter 3

CHOOSING THE GUN-DOG PROSPECT

❧❧

THE CHOICE of a prospect should be a matter of great concern to the beginner and particularly to one who plans to keep only one dog. For then it is doubly important that the youngster selected should show promise. A good start in any campaign is a battle half won.

Too many times I have heard self-styled authorities as they indicated a certain puppy in a very young litter scampering about the kennel yard: "*There* is the best puppy in the litter. It will make the best performer in the field."

Such statements are nothing short of absurd, for it is humanly impossible to make such a choice with any degree of certainty. These statements are almost always based on personal tastes. The puppy thus indicated is more than likely marked or conformed to suit the chooser's fancy; he may carry himself merrily or may show a greater amount of precocity than his brothers or sisters.

Boldness in the kennel yard and at a tender age does not necessarily presage anything, for the smallest, weakest puppy in the three-month-old litter may develop into the most apt pupil and the best-looking dog. The smallest puppy at birth may, with proper care, develop into the largest dog, while the strongest and most promising youngster might, if mistreated, be most disappointing at maturity.

So, as the selection of a very young puppy is a matter of catch-as-catch-can or hit-or-miss judgment, it is best to delay the choice until the natural qualities of the individuals become evident.

The four most popular breeds of pointing dogs from which the selection can be made are the pointer, the English setter, the Irish setter, and the German short-haired pointer, the latter somewhat of a newcomer but growing in popularity. Another pointing breed that is attracting attention is the Brittany spaniel. Then there are the Gordon setter, the pointing griffon, now seldom seen in American hunting fields, and the Weimaraner, a breed just getting a start here.

Experience has taught us that, as a general rule, the first two breeds mentioned make the best field performers, so we would advise the beginner to choose a young pointer or English setter as his prospect.

Preference between these two breeds is merely a matter of personal opinion, as the main difference lies in the color and length of coat. The pointer fancier contends that this breed develops faster, takes to training more kindly, and is easier to control. He also advances that the pointer's short coat allows him to withstand excessive heat better and prevents him from becoming loaded down with burs, which become matted in the longer hair of the setter. He asserts that the pointer is possessed of a more even temperament and his spirit is not so easily broken under the application of mild force in training.

The admirer of the setter maintains that his abundant coat allows him to do better work in cold, wet weather and gives him a decided advantage in rough country infested with briars and brambles. They also hold that the setter has a more lovable disposition than the pointer, more personality, as it were, is more loyal, and generally is possessed of more dash and energy.

It has been the writer's experience that while the pointer develops faster as a breed and reaches the state of perfection in training sooner and with less effort on the part of the trainer, he is also more apt to forget his training between seasons and have to have part of it done over. The setter, on the other hand, while slower to reach that state of perfection is more inclined to retain it throughout the years without renewed effort on the part of the trainer. This has been my experience and that of many others.

Personally, I have no preference in the two breeds. There are good and poor individuals in both breeds. There are pointers that will face the roughest going in the worst weather, and setters that will maintain a slashing gait on hot, dry days. The setter's coat can be trimmed to such an extent that burs will give him little trouble and there are pointers whose loyalty is unsurpassed.

So, in the final analysis, the choice of a breed boils down to a matter of personal preference. A good bird dog is a good bird dog, regardless of the length of his hair.

But, by all means, choose your prospect from well-bred stock. A pedigreed puppy is just as easy to keep as one of unknown lineage. Do not, however, purchase a dog simply because he has a fancy pedigree, for fashionable breeding is not always a certain pathway to bird-dog supremacy. See that he comes from a line of well-bred and *proven* field performers and you can be reasonably sure that he will have, at least, some good natural hunting-dog qualities.

Breeding history proves that certain bloodlines crossed on certain other bloodlines produce a good percentage of high-class field dogs. It also records that the blending of certain lines produces, with fair regularity, general characteristics that include both faults and good qualities.

It would be well for the beginner to choose his puppy from a known nick, i.e., a line of breeding that has previously produced good dogs. If this is impracticable, it would be advisable for him to study the general characteristics of the dogs that are close up in the puppy's pedigree and ascertain as much as possible about the faults and good qualities of the youngster's ancestors.

The matter of the desirability of certain blends in breeding requires much study of pedigree and performance. The law of inheritance presents a science in itself, and the writer will make no attempt to delve into its intricacies here, but the beginner would be wise to submit the pedigree of his prospective purchase to some student of breeding before closing the transaction.

Bird dogs have come to have a recognized value. It is obvious that a dog of known pedigree is of more value than one from what is commonly known as cold-blooded parentage. But aside from the intrinsic value of the animal, it is sound reasoning to expect a well-bred youngster, coming from a line of high-class performers, to prove of more value in the field than one whose ancestry is clouded. It costs no more to keep a well-bred dog, and the accompanying pride of ownership is worth far more than the difference in the original cost.

While coloration has no direct bearing on a dog's natural abilities, this matter should be given serious consideration by the beginner, as it may later have an indirect influence on the dog's field education.

The question of the color of the markings of the prospect can only be settled through personal preference and is relatively unimportant. The most popular color combinations in pointers are white and liver, white and orange, white and black, and occasionally solid liver and solid black individuals are found. In setters the preference runs to white, black and tan, white and black, and white and orange. Blue beltons and orange beltons are especially desired by bench-show fanciers, while the combination of white and chestnut has but few champions.

No matter what color combination you choose, be sure that your puppy will be easily discernible in cover. To bring about this effect the greater portion of his body should be white. This does not mean that body markings or large patches or spots are to be frowned upon entirely, for an evenly marked dog is generally easy to see.

A dog whose body is mostly white, however, stands out in bold relief and it is easier to locate him when he is in high cover. Dogs colored with a heavy bluish cast are particularly hard to see on a dull, hazy day, for they have a way of blending in with the cover and becoming a part of the landscape. A dog whose body is almost covered with liver or black patches is exceedingly hard to see in thick, heavy cover, while one of the belton types, or, in pointers, roan, has the effect of fading away in the distance even in open country.

Occasionally there are some distinctive markings that prove quite attractive and serve to make the dog easily identified at a distance. A notable example was National Champion McTyre, a pointer that had a liver stripe running down the full length of one leg. Another striking example was National Champion Rapid Transit. The right side of this dog was almost white, faintly clouded with liver ticks. His left side was heavily marked by a long saddle of liver. When the dog made a left quartering cast he presented an entirely different picture from that offered when he ran with his right side in plain view of the observer. So striking was the contrast that one almost got the effect of watching two different dogs as he hunted out the birdy places on both sides of the course. Distinctive markings, from a standpoint of instant identification, are desirable, but a smoothly and evenly marked bird dog is a thing of beauty indeed and is preferred by the majority.

Size sometimes plays an important part in a dog's performance. A small bird dog is at a distinct handicap in crashing through high and heavy cover and sometimes tires more easily when his weight is insufficient to carry him through. A large dog is more easily seen in cover or the open, but, on the other hand, his gait may not be as pleasing and he may not possess the dash and punch of the smaller individual. So it is best to try to strike a happy medium and select a prospect that promises to develop enough bone and muscle to enable him to bore through heavy areas without distress and, at the same time, be small enough to handle himself gracefully and easily.

Gun dogs vary a good deal in size, and maturity weights ranging from thirty-five to fifty-five pounds are not uncommon. While dogs of good size have an advantage, often the smaller dogs make up for this deficiency by possessing a superabundance of energy and courage. Sioux, LaBesita and Pin Money were all small setter bitches that took the measure of the best field-trial contenders of their day, Sand Line, Ireland's Greymist, Mingo, and Norias Annie were small bitches with brilliant records, and Hillbright Susanna, diminutive setter bitch, was somewhat of a sensation in field trials.

The action, or manner of moving, of a prospect should be carefully considered by the beginner. After all, you intend to develop the young dog for your own pleasure and want to enjoy his companionship to the fullest degree, both in and out of the hunting season. A dog that carries himself gracefully, merrily, and with a smoothness of stride that is devoid of friction is beautiful to watch in the field and presents a thrilling study in effortless action. The hunting season is short, at best, but many hours of genuine pleasure can be derived from watching an attractively moving dog in the field on recreational jaunts. Choose a dog that carries a high head and a merry tail, that sweeps along with a smooth, frictionless but high stride, and your field pleasure will be enhanced A low or "dead" tail detracts from the dog's carriage. A high-headed dog is more pleasing to look at than one that carries his head below the level of his back.

I have seen practically all of the major circuit, field-trial dogs of the past quarter of a century and have judged most of them. Three dogs stand out boldly in my memory as the personifications of beauty in action. These are National Champion Mississippi Zev, which I believe to be outstandingly above all other dogs I have seen in this respect; the setter bitch Halworthy's Kate; and the pointer bitch, Mingo. All were simply poetry in motion, and, as such, fairly *demanded* the attention of every official who judged them.

Then there is the matter of sex. While there are exceptions to the rule, the two genders generally have distinctly different characteristics aside from those of a sexual nature. Bitches are generally more easily satisfied with confinement than males and are usually more affectionate. They are, in many instances, more tractable than males, but this factor may be affected by a greater degree of timidness. More careful handling is generally required for them, however, as their constitutional peculiarities sometimes greatly affect their temperaments. Moreover, they must be closely confined during periods when they are in season, and this sometimes presents a problem to the amateur owner who is not properly equipped. This, of course, may be eliminated by spaying, but we would never advise this operation, as it is in direct interference with the natural functions of the dog's organs. Spaying generally has the tendency to make the bitch become listless and dull and sometimes destroys entirely her ambition to hunt.

Dogs differ greatly in disposition. Some are bold and fearless, while others are timid and shy. Some are affectionate, while others are indifferent; some sociable, some quarrelsome. Try to choose as your prospect a puppy that shows no tendency to timidness but that indicates a desire to cultivate the friendship of his master. Avoid one of a quarrelsome nature, for you may be constantly in trouble with your neighbor over his actions. And steer clear of the one that possesses a nervous, high-strung, excitable temperament that will not allow him to look at mankind through confiding eyes. A man-shy puppy is a source of inconvenience and embarrassment, to say the least, but this fault can in time be corrected by careful handling and lavish affection.

Look for the puppy that appears to be glad he is alive, that seems willing to accept your friendship and return your attentions in kind; confidently stands his own ground when faced by strange sights and strange people, has an inquisitive nature, and seems to want to learn about things.

In him you will have found a youngster that will take to training kindly and one that can be developed into a pleasant gunning companion.

Chapter 4

CARE

❦

DOGS are in many respects like human beings. Their well-being demands more than the mere provision of proper food, shelter, and sanitation. They thrive on attention, companionship, and affection. While these qualities should not be provided in such abundant quantities as to develop the shooting-dog prospect into a spoiled and pampered pet, nevertheless, they are essential to the dog's rapid development in training.

He should be kept in comfortable quarters that make for congenial surroundings; he should be given proper food and in such quantities necessary to keep him in excellent condition; and prompt and effective attention should be given to the minor physical ailments to which he will be subjected. Withal, he should be given the love and affection of his master.

Good care is essential to proper condition. And proper condition is necessary if best training results are to be obtained.

Kenneling

Dogs kept out of doors are much less subject to illness from exposure than those that spend most of their days and all of their nights inside the house. If, however, it is impractical to build a kennel for him, he should be provided with a rug or other bedding to sleep on at night. This bedding should be aired during the daytime and thoroughly cleaned once a week.

A good substantial kennel should be provided. There are many types, from the simple kerosene or molasses barrel to the elaborate structures containing two or three compartments. The barrel type is cheap and quite simple of construction. And it can solve the kennel problem for the man who intends to keep only one dog. It will serve well as a temporary kennel, but most sportsmen desire something of a more substantial nature. I have used one in my kennel yard for the past six years as an extra kennel, and it is still in good condition. It is particularly useful in summer months and solves the problem of kenneling at the summer home or camp during the summer vacation.

Secure an ordinary watertight kerosene or molasses barrel. Clean it as thoroughly as possible. Then burn a quantity of shavings or excelsior in it to eliminate the smell. From a strip of two-by-four timber saw two braces some ten inches longer than the diameter of the barrel. Cut depressions in these braces into which the barrel can fit, and place one under each end. Hold these braces in place by securing together with strips.

This type of kennel may be used temporarily or as a permanent home. During the summer cooling shade should be provided. A triangular shed can be placed over it to keep out the rain and further protect it. This can also be removed and used as a windbreaker or to provide shade. A strip of canvas tacked to the top of the barrel and weighted should hang down over the entrance to serve as a door and to break the wind.

If no shed is available, an awning may be provided by stretching a strip of canvas from the open end of the barrel to two posts driven into the ground some three or four feet in front. If desired the barrel may be fastened down with wire. If the barrel is to be used as a winter kennel, a narrow strip should be nailed across the lower part of the entrance to prevent the bedding from falling out. In the summertime no bedding is necessary. This type of kennel is comfortable for one dog and is quickly and easily cleaned.

While this kennel is satisfactory in a good many respects, many sportsmen prefer to give their dogs housing of a more ample character. There is a wide range in the types of kennel used. Some are makeshift affairs, which provide little more than shelter. Others are of elaborate construction, decorated with fancy folderols and useless doodads. Whatever type you decide upon, see that it is built with comfort as the main consideration. Double boarding, reinforced between with some good insulation material, should be employed.

Nothing contributes more to the discomfort of the dog than fleas or parasites of the skin. In order to combat these pests, the kennel must be kept clean at all times. It should be thoroughly cleaned and disinfected at least once a week and the bedding changed weekly. Fleas do not find cedar shavings attractive, and a quantity of these shavings sprinkled in the bedding have a deterring effect. I use cedar shavings as bedding (nothing else), but its cost is rather high. Good coarse wheat or rice straw provides more warmth for winter use. The development of DDT has just about solved the flea problem. DDT sprays of 5 per-cent strength are highly recommended. It can be obtained easily and is not expensive.

If the dog is to be kept on a chain he will be allowed more exercise if he is permitted to run along a wire. Drive two stakes in the ground, one directly in front of his kennel, the other some thirty or forty feet in front of it. Slip an iron ring on a smooth wire and stretch the wire on the ground between the two stakes, attaching it to them. Snap the dog's swivel-chain to the iron ring and he can secure considerable exercise by running in the space provided.

However, if at all possible he should be given the freedom of a kennel yard, for confinement on a wire is sure to become irksome and may affect his disposition. A good kennel yard may cost considerable money but will prove much more satisfactory to dog and owner.

Some dogs have the disposition to dig and are constantly trying to escape from confinement in this manner. This danger can be eliminated by stapling a strip of chicken wire, twelve to eighteen inches in width, to the kennel-fence baseboard on the inside of the kennel, and staking the outer edge to the ground. The dog discovers that he cannot dig next to the fence and will soon abandon these troublesome tactics.

There are other types of kennel breakers who obtain their liberty by fence climbing. This practice can be stopped by installing a "hangover" along the top of the fence. Nail to the tops of the fence posts, or along the side near the top, strips of one-by-four, twelve to eighteen inches in length in a horizontal position or at a slight upward angle, and extending over the interior of the kennel yard. Over these strips stretch poultry wire, nailing it to the wood and attaching one edge to the fence.

The sizes of kennel yards vary with the amount of space available. They should be as large as space will permit and, if possible, one corner at least should extend under a tree in order that shade be secured. If no trees or shrubs are available, shade can be obtained by placing a wide, low table in the yard. He will enjoy it in all seasons, as he can lie on it to sun himself in cool weather, and the ground underneath it will afford him comfort in warm weather. The planting of grapevines and other climbing plants along the south and west sides of the kennel fence will add to his comfort.

The kennel yard should be cleaned daily and occasionally spaded up and treated with wood ashes or a light lime spread. A clean kennel yard is the best protection against worms. Fleas and lice thrive in sand, so black dirt or clay is the best ground for a kennel yard. It should be well drained, for no dog can be comfortable in a muddy yard.

A type of kennel sanitation has recently come into popularity. This is done by placing the entire kennel yard on wire, and keeping both house and yard some two to three feet off the ground. The yard, which is built around an elevated house, is not very difficult to prepare.

Feeding

The alteration of conditions and modes of living, accompanying the advance of civilization, has made marked changes in canine diet. Essentially a carnivorous animal, the dog in recent years has become more nearly omnivorous, as he has been forced to change his feeding habits to varying conditions. This, fortunately, he has been able to do without loss of size, bone, stamina, or natural instincts.

The condition of the working dog depends, in a large measure, upon the manner in which he is fed, and hence the matter of feeding is of major importance. It has been said, "We are what we eat." This statement may be even more applicable to dogs. Proteins, carbohydrates, fats, and minerals represent the basis of the balanced diet, and the balanced ration must contain these elements in such proper proportion as to facilitate prompt digestion, assimilation, and final expulsion of indigestible residue. Yet there are other elements that play a most important part in food utilization.

These are the vitamins, which vitalize a ration, transforming it from a "dead" food to the proper maintenance of a healthy organism. Without vitamins no food can sustain a healthful life, yet vitamins alone are not a sufficiency. A really balanced ration is one that contains all the health-building properties in the proper proportion.

As the dog is of a carnivorous nature, the principal source of his food is obtained from the animal kingdom, i.e., milk, eggs, meat, glandular organs (liver, kidney, etc.), animal fats, and bone. Not only do these possess essential food value but, in the fresh, raw state, they prevent the diet from becoming deficient in vitamin content.

Dogs, however, have learned, through necessity sometimes, to adapt themselves to a varied diet and most of them will now thrive on limited quantities of certain vegetables, fruits, and whole-wheat bread in conjunction with animal foods. This is fortunate, as these commodities are easily obtainable, provide bulk and roughage, and guard against vitamin shortage.

Beef and mutton are the best meats for the dog's diet. Pork should never be fed.

Of the vegetables, carrots, spinach, turnip greens, tomatoes, onions, cabbage and lettuce are preferred.

The major portion of the dog's diet is most generally well cooked. This is the most convenient way to prepare it, but raw food is better for him if he can be induced to eat it. Some dogs refuse to eat raw vegetables, but persistence will generally bring them around to it. However, cooked vegetables, served in their own juices, are all right.

Great advances have been made in the commercial manufacture of dog food. This ready-to-serve food has solved the problem for many dog fanciers, and the dog-food industry is one of the largest in this country. These foods are blended in such manner as to provide a balanced ration, and many thousands of hunting dogs are now kept in good condition on them and little else. Meat, of course, is extremely high these days and difficult to obtain. However, I am a great believer in feeding as much meat as possible, particularly to working dogs.

I have seen the feeding of meat pay big dividends in bird-dog and fox-hound field-trial contenders. When Dr. Frank Lahey, famous Boston surgeon, was active in bird-dog field trials his dogs were fed raw meat daily. His best-known color bearer was the pointer, Junedale Allie. If she was being conditioned for competitions in which the heats were of one hour's duration, Allie was fed one pound of hamburger meat daily. If the heats were to be two hours, she received two pounds, and if she was being pointed for the endurance-championship stakes of three hours, her daily diet contained three pounds of meat. She usually finished her heats as strongly as she started out.

In recent years I have seen considerable written material about the needlessness of giving large raw bones to dogs, the writers contending that they get sufficient bone meal in commercial dog foods and are prone to swallow large chunks of bone, which might cause trouble. Nevertheless, my dogs are given every good beef or mutton bone I can get.

Table scraps, too, should be added to the dog's meal, provided they do not contain fish or chicken bones or a considerable amount of potatoes. Always save the water in which meat and vegetables are cooked, and mix with the dog's food. The garbage man seldom carries a heavy load away from our house . . . and my dogs are generally in good condition.

Don't overfeed. Experience will teach you just how much your dog needs. Satisfy his hunger but keep him keen.

Feeding raw eggs is just a case of wasting eggs. Soft-boiled eggs should be added to the weak or undernourished dog's diet several times a week, but don't give them to him raw.

Puppies should be fed small amounts and often. Never allow them to gorge themselves at one time to the extent that discomfort results. At weaning time they can be changed to fresh cow's milk and frequent helpings of finely chopped raw beef and raw liver. Cod-liver oil and fruit juices are beneficial. For the first few months their diet should consist mainly of fresh raw milk, raw beef with the fat that comes with it, raw liver and kidney, with increasing amounts of commercial dog food mixed in. Puppies should be fed three meals a day when they are from three to nine months of age. After that, two meals will be sufficient.

After he has passed the puppy stage, two meals a day are all that are necessary for the dog, a light breakfast and a good meal at night. The amount of food necessary can be ascertained by observation. Give him all he will eat at night, but remove any leftover food from the kennel.

A pan of sweet, sour, or buttermilk, into which a quantity of finely crumbled shredded-wheat biscuit has been placed, makes a fine breakfast. The evening meal should be more substantial, consisting of beef, heart, lamb, or horse meat, with vegetables. If this isn't practical, most commercial dog foods provide a balanced ration that is sufficient.

Some trainers feed once a day only, giving the dog all he will eat at night. They hold this is best for the working dog, as it gives him time to assimilate his food and prevents a full stomach from making him sluggish, with discomfort in the field next day. As it requires some eighteen to twenty-four hours for food to pass through the intestinal tract, the working dog should never be given a heavy meal at breakfast, but I prefer to give him a light feed early in the morning before a hard day in the field.

Regularity in feeding hours can be easily turned into a valuable asset to training. Approach the kennel with the food at the same time each morning and night. The young dog will come to anticipate these visits, and his accuracy in gauging the time for them will be surprising. Accompany the feeding trip to the kennel with considerable noise, such as hammering on a board, the banging of tin pans, etc. The puppy will come to associate strange noises with his mealtime and will not long be afraid. Then introduce a blast from a small-caliber pistol or rifle as the feeding-time signal. The gun should be fired some 40 to 50 yards from the kennel at first, gradually reducing the distance. After the puppy has become accustomed to this noise, and shows no fear of it, fire a .410-gauge shotgun as a signal. Finally graduate to a 20-gauge shotgun, and if the puppy shows no fear of this, and he shouldn't, you may rest assured that he will not show signs of gun-shyness when his education in the field begins. The employment of this method is no guarantee that the youngster will not become gun-shy later on if careless tactics are used, but it is mighty good insurance against this fault.

Wash your pans and dishes immediately after feeding, as these utensils must be kept scrupulously clean.

A dog may go several days without food and still not suffer a serious blow to his general condition, provided he has access to a plentiful supply of fresh water. A bucket or earthen crock of fresh water should be kept before him at all times, for an insufficient water supply promotes an unhealthy condition, particularly of the skin. Earthen vessels make the best water containers, as they do not rust, can be easily cleaned, and do not tip over so readily.

Washing

Occasional washing is an aid to good health and cleanliness. In warm weather, a washing now and then helps; in cold weather washing is somewhat risky, and thorough grooming is preferred. Any good germicidal soap is satisfactory, but care should be taken to keep the soapy water out of the dog's eyes and ears. The dog should be rinsed as often as necessary to clear the coat and skin of every particle of soap. He should be thoroughly dried before he is allowed out of doors. Be sure to see that the ears and feet are dry. The dog should be rubbed thoroughly dry with rough towels or clean, dry gunny sacks.

Frequent brushing of the coat is really more important than washing, particularly in cold weather. Brushing cleans the coat of foreign matter, dirt, and filth, and stimulates the growth of healthy hair, promoting an attractive sheen or glisten through proper circulation.

Immunization against Distemper

It has been frequently said that a dog is only half a dog until he has had distemper. This statement could have been taken literally several years ago, and even now it has a truthful ring. But recently several vaccines and serums have been developed that cope with this dread disease in a fairly successful manner. We do not say that these treatments are completely effective in all cases but we do not hesitate to recommend that every owner of a young dog consult a competent veterinarian in this regard and accept his recommendation. "An ounce of prevention is worth a pound of cure," and that "pound of cure" may not save your dog if he is stricken with distemper.

Naming the Youngster

As the use of the puppy's kennel name will be frequently employed in both yard and field training, and will remain with him through his lifetime, it is essential that the appellation given him be one that he will readily recognize. To accomplish this, the shorter the name the better. Words of one syllable are much to be preferred over long ones, and those with a sharp, crisp sound are best. A short name, with a distinctive sound, is not so easily confused with others, and a more ready response is effected.

For males such kennel names as Joe, Jack, Jim, John, Tom, Sam, Buck, Jake, Rip, Rap, Kent, Beau, and Frank are in common use, and for bitches such names as Nell, Kate, Flirt, Fly, Madge, Mary, Belle, Becky, Jane, and Bess are in high favor.

See that the name of your dog is a short one, and that he learns it. He may be recorded in the annals of registered dogdom under a somewhat long, high-sounding name that denotes his ancestry. This is all well, and favored by many, but a short kennel name for everyday use should also be given him.

Registering the Dog

It is assumed that the beginner has secured a young dog that is eligible to registration in the various stud books, i.e., coming from pedigreed parentage. After he has survived the puppy-disease period, no time should be lost in registering him.

The registration of the dog provides a permanent record of his breeding, ownership, age, and markings and discourages fraud and misrepresentation. The *Field Dog Stud Book*, operated by the American Field Publishing Co., Chicago, Ill., is the most popular registration record among bird-dog fanciers, although the book registers all breeds. The weekly registrations of this medium are published in the regular issues of the *American Field Magazine*, giving the public opportunity to protest against any evidence of error or fraud. The registration certificate is issued later.

The first volume of the *Field Dog Stud Book* was issued in 1901, with 675 dogs registered. The book has increased in volume annually and has proven its worth as an index to bird-dog breeding and performance. The first dog to be registered in the F.D.S.B. was the setter bitch Our Lillian, bred by Jackson-Denmark Kennels, Denmark, Tenn., and owned by Alexander McLachlan, New Franklin, Mo. Our Lillian was sired by Champion Joe Cumming, and her dam was Marie Girard. Since those early days Mr. McLachlan has bred a number of good ones, among them being the winning pointer derbies, Taneycomo and Little Mary McLachlan.

Application blanks to registry in the F.D.S.B. may be secured from the American Field Publishing Company. Full details concerning the filling out of these applications are contained upon the backs of the blanks.

Names for registration must not exceed three words or initials. Many owners prefer to register their dogs under long names that indicate the families from which they sprung. These names are sometimes confusing and not as distinctive as they might be. It is best to choose a short, attractive name that will carry a significance in the event that the puppy should develop into a winner. It is not necessary to include the dog's kennel name in his registered name. For instance, National Champion Doughboy's kennel name was Lewis; National Champion Rapid Transit's kennel name was Mike; Mike was also the kennel name of the famous setter, Eugene's Ghost. Champion Ghost of Joyeuse answered to the kennel name of Nick, while the pointer Mad Anthony responded to the name Buck. By some quirk of circumstance, the kennel name of double-amateur Champion Bill's Bob was Sam, while his kennel mate, futurity winner Muscle Shoals Sam, answered when the name Jim was called.

But regardless of the name you select, be sure to register your dog. It enhances his value and that of his progeny. Breeding history can only be preserved through registration of individuals, and knowledge of the characteristics and performances of these individuals and their ancestors is the most valuable information available to students who are constantly striving to improve the breeds.

Another all-breed stud book is that of the American Kennel Club, New York City.

External Parasites

During the warm summer months, the dog is constantly exposed to the attacks of fleas, flies, and other parasites that cause him discomfort. His well-being demands that his owner make every effort to combat these pests.

The kennel yard must be kept scrupulously clean. Every few weeks it will be well to scatter unslaked lime over the ground and wet it down thoroughly. The dog should be removed from the kennel and kept elsewhere for five or six hours until the lime has cooled. Fences and buildings should be whitewashed occasionally and a little creolin mixed in with the calcimine to good advantage. Creolin solutions should be poured in the cracks and crevices of the floors and walls, and the boxes and kennel houses should be frequently scrubbed with a one-hundred-to-one solution of any of the creosote preparations. The development of DDT and its various solutions makes this problem now fairly simple, particularly for the man who plans to keep only one or two dogs. This subject is discussed at greater length in a later chapter.

However, for the larger kennel dips of a disinfecting and antiseptic nature are important. In the hot summer months, dogs that are kept confined in kennel yards should be dipped every week in a sulphur solution. This dip, which not only destroys vermin but is beneficial to the skin, is made as follows:

Fill a fifty-gallon barrel about three quarters full of water. Empty two one-pound cans of Lewis Lye into an earthen crock or vessel. Over the mixture pour several cans of water, stir until the lye is dissolved. Into this mixture, pour five pounds of sulphur that has been thoroughly screened to eliminate the lumps. Stir until the mixture turns a reddish color and dissolve in a bucket of hot water. Pour this in the barrel and add one quart of *crude* carbolic acid or three ounces of commercial sulphuric acid. (Some trainers do not like to use acid in this dip and it can be eliminated without impairing the efficiency of the dip too much.) After the solution has been used a number of times, a small glass of kerosene added before dipping each dog will help. The dip will not last more than two or three weeks in hot weather without developing a rather foul odor. It should be replaced with fresh material.

In dipping the dog, place his hindquarters in the barrel first. Make sure that the mixture does not get into his eyes or ears. Hold him with one hand and use a sponge to wet him thoroughly.

If a top is kept on the barrel the mixture will last longer.

If there are several dogs to be dipped, it is well to provide a drainboard so that he can be placed on it directly after lifting him from the barrel. The mixture will drip from his body and run back into the barrel. After dipping the dog, either dry him thoroughly with a rough towel or gunny sack, or turn him loose on a grassy lawn and let him run himself dry. Watch him carefully to see that he doesn't wallow in dirt. Be sure he is dry before placing him in the kennel or turning him loose.

This solution is excellent to keep the dog free of fleas and ticks. Sometimes lice are extremely hard to remove from young dogs. These pests generally infest the ears and the back of the neck. They can be destroyed by using a preparation of one part of skimmed milk and two parts of kerosene. Heat the milk, mix with the kerosene, and mix thoroughly. Apply the solution, after it has cooled, with a stiff brush, rubbing it in briskly. Two or three applications may be necessary to remove the pests, which should be combed out.

Chapter 5

TRAINING EQUIPMENT

❧

BEFORE serious field training is started it is best that the puppy be taught a few simple commands, thus bringing him under some semblance of control. He should know his name, should come when called, should feel at ease when placed on a lead, and should be familiar with whistle and voice signals.

In order to teach him even these simple things the trainer should secure certain pieces of equipment. These are a lead, a whistle, a whip, and a check cord.

The Lead

There are any number of different kinds of leads on the market. Some are light, flimsy affairs that are unsuitable; others are heavy affairs too bunglesome for our purposes. The proper lead for a bird dog is simply a stout leather strap, some six feet long and one half to three quarters of an inch wide. It should have a loop in one end to serve as a handgrip and a swivel-snap at the other for attachment to the dog's collar. Many prefer one end to be made so as to provide a sliding-loop collar, which can be easily slipped on or off the dog's neck over his head. Either is satisfactory. A chain is all right but rather hard on the hands. In the succeeding chapters, the lead will be known as the short lead.

The Whistle

Whistles are made in various forms. The most common are made of bone, metal, or rubber composition. Some produce a smooth blast, while others have a cork ball in the barrel that produces a rolling blast. The latter is in high favor. Whichever you choose, be sure that the whistle is loud enough to be heard at considerable distance.

A large whistle has a sufficient length of mouthpiece, which allows it to be retained in the mouth without assistance from the hand. Metal whistles are liable to chap the lips in cold weather, and for this reason hard-rubber composition is to be preferred. A convenient way to carry a whistle is to attach it to a buckskin lace or stout cord hung around the neck. It is then always in place and easily accessible.

The whistle has several functions. It is used to attract the dog's attention, to turn him when quartering, to bring him in, and to make him increase his pace and range. The single blast will serve for the first three purposes. When it is used merely to attract the dog's attention, the command that follows is sufficient. One long blast is used to turn the dog from his cast, while a similar blast followed at intervals by others is the signal for him to come in to the trainer. Two short sharp blasts are generally employed as a signal to increase the pace and extend the range. After the dog has become stanch and steady to shot and wing, a short, soft blast is a good signal to send him on after the birds have been flushed and the gun reloaded, or to send him in to relocate if the birds have run on him.

The Whip

Whips also vary in construction and size. Many of them are merely cruel agencies of punishment and have no place in dog training. It must be remembered by the beginner that it is not always the amount of punishment that does the dog good. First, he must know what he is being punished for, and punishment should *never* be administered until you are sure that the dog is aware of the reason for it. Then it should be employed only as a badge of authority to show the dog that you are the master and must be obeyed. The part the whip is to play in dog training depends largely upon the individual dog. Some are highly sensitive and respond quickly to mild correction with the voice. In these cases, it is best to leave the whip out of the picture. Otherwise, you court the making of a man-shy dog. Others are bold, fearless, and headstrong, and more drastic measures must be adopted to bring them into hand. It is with these that the use of the whip may be resorted to when need for correction arises.

Always remember to use the whip sparingly. Its abuse may result in a spoiled dog. Generally a light, limber switch will serve the purpose to engender the fear of punishment, which, after all, is the real function of the whip. However, one cannot always secure the switch at the moment when it is most needed, so it is best to provide yourself with a serviceable whip that can be tucked out of sight in your clothing but secured at a moment's notice.

A good, cheap whip can be made in the following manner: Secure three pieces of leather approximately three quarters of an inch wide and about two and one-half feet long. Lap one piece over at one end so that a small loop large enough to slip a thong through is formed. Taper each piece, both in width and thickness so that, when they are laid one upon the other, the width narrows from three fourths of an inch at the top to about three eighths of an inch at the bottom, and the thickness diminishes from one-half to less than one-fourth inch. Stitch together with harness thread, a row of stitches down each side and one in the middle. Allow one piece to form a short lash at the end. Slip a short buckskin thong through the small loop, slip a small snap on the thong, tie it in proper length to allow the thong to slip over your hand and hang from the wrist. And the whip is completed.

This whip can be made to serve several purposes. The thong at the end allows it to be carried on the wrist; the snap on the thong allows its use as a lead; it is a good riding whip; it is not heavy enough to inflict severe punishment to the dog, and is flexible enough to be rolled up and placed in the hunting-coat pocket when not in use. Any leather worker can make it at small cost.

Whenever it becomes necessary to use the whip, the trainer should remember to control himself and refrain from giving vent to his feelings. The whip should be applied lightly, with just enough force to convince the dog that he is being punished. The trainer should remain calm, speaking to the dog in a moderate tone, diminishing the force of the strokes and lowering his voice until the whip is barely being laid on the dog's back. The dog should be made to drop and remain in this position for a few minutes after the punishment has been administered, the trainer speaking to him in a low voice the while. Then, after a few pats, the dog should be sent on. He will probably go about his work good-naturedly, although realizing that he has been punished for the commission of an error. And never punish him until you have caught him in the act of committing that error.

Experienced trainers know when and how to apply the

whip. Novices often abuse the practice of whipping because they do not know how far to go and when to stop, and so we discourage the use of the whip as long as milder methods of correction will suffice. If you are to use a whip, see that your dog is not shy of it. Use it as a lead frequently. Acquaint him with the fact that it, in itself, is harmless by laying it on his back in a good-natured manner occasionally. He should never think of it as an instrument of punishment except when he commits an error.

The Check Cord

The check cord is one of the most important accessories in bird-dog training. In the entire course, there are but few steps in which it cannot be employed to good advantage. Through its judicious use the dog can be brought to realize that he must be under control at all times and must work for his master.

Check cords vary in length according to the purpose they are to serve. For general use, twenty to thirty feet is sufficiently long. Stout, tightly braided window-sash cord is excellent material to use, as the cord should be light yet strong. A coat of oil will improve it. To one end attach a swivel-snap, so that the cord can be quickly attached to the dog's collar. The other end should not be knotted, but should be tightly bound with fine wire or waxed harness thread. This will allow the end to slide through the cover without retarding the dog's gait.

The Spike Collar

This is a book for the beginner—the simon-pure amateur —so the less said about the spike or so-called force collar the better. The only reason for mentioning it here is the fact that these collars are in existence and in use by most experienced trainers. In the hands of the inexperienced they can become instruments of torture, and I have no hesitancy in advising beginners to let them alone. Dogs can be forced to do things through more humane methods and without incurring the risk of permanently breaking the individual's spirit.

Collars

Every dog should be provided with a collar. These also vary in type and style from the wide, brass-studded choker to the thin buckskin strap. For the bird dog, a simple, plain leather-strap collar, equipped with a ring to which may be attached a chain, lead, or check cord, and a name plate with the name and address of the owner thereon, is all that is necessary, and is in better taste than one adorned by a lot of fancy ornaments. The round, or rolled, collar is also serviceable and attractive.

Chapter 6

EARLY LESSONS

The Use of Training Equipment

❧

THE FIRST THING a puppy should be taught is to know his name. Select a short name for him and use it every time you address him. He will soon learn to recognize it. When he responds to the name and comes to you, reward him with a small tidbit or a caress. When out for a walk with him, it is a good idea to carry along some small morsels of food and frequently call him to you, giving him one as a reward.

To Lead

The next step is to accustom him to a lead. Teaching the dog to lead is a simple matter, but before you start let him become familiar with a collar and a chain. If you have more than one puppy, put collars on all of them. After they have become accustomed to the collars, tie short pieces of colored rags to the collars. The puppies will tug against these streamers in play, which aids in accustoming the puppy to an attachment on his neck. After a while of this, see that the collar is tight enough so that it will not slip over his head, then chain him in a comfortable place where he cannot become tangled up or choke himself, and leave him to his own devices for an hour or so each day. He will soon stop his efforts to get away and realize that the chain or lead means that he no longer has his liberty.

After a few days of this, attach a short lead to his collar, call him to your side and start for a stroll. He may desire to remain behind and will pull or plunge against the lead. Continue your walk, however, pulling him along with you and he will soon learn that it is useless to resist. When he ceases to struggle, pet him and encourage him. You will soon be able to lead him anywhere. Avoid taking him into strange surroundings for a while, however, and lead him around the place until he has become thoroughly accustomed to having his freedom restricted. Talk to him in a low, kind tone as you stroll along, and pet him frequently.

Teaching Him to Come When Called

Learning to come when called by voice or whistle is next. Around the kennel and yard, the puppy will readily respond when his name is called and generally come to you when ordered. He does this because he wants to play or expects to be rewarded. But when he becomes interested in something else he may pay little attention when ordered to "Come here." It is then that he must be given a lesson in obedience and made to realize that he *must* come to you promptly and under any circumstances when his name is called.

Take the dog out of the kennel yard. Attach a check cord to his collar and allow him to have a short romp. When his attention is attracted by something, call him by name and give the command "Come here." If he responds, pat him and allow him to continue his romp, calling him to you at intervals.

Presently he will become tired of having his pleasure interfered with, and will refuse to come when ordered. Grasp the end of the check cord, repeat the command "Come here," and give the cord a sharp jerk. He will probably try to resist, but keep giving the command, and a few sharp jerks will bring him to you. If he does not come, pull him in to you. Reward him with tidbits and caresses. Repeat this several times, and he will begin to realize that he *must* come when called.

Don't allow a lesson to last too long. This one can be repeated several times a day, but having him come to you three or four times in one session is sufficient. If he should sulk and remain with you, don't become discouraged.

Place him in his kennel. He will probably welcome the return, for he wants to get away from you. Leave the kennel gate open, and allow him to get settled in his bunk. Then call his name, giving the command "Come here." When he fails to respond, jerk sharply on the cord and draw him to you. Reward him and send him back to the kennel. He will soon discover that resistance is useless and will come to you promptly when called.

It is a good idea to leave the cord on him for an hour or so at a time while you are doing odd jobs about the yard. When he does not expect it, give the command "Come here" and then jerk the cord *lightly*. This will remind him that you still have control over him and that he must obey. Never fail to reward him when he responds, even if only with a pat or two.

You should also work him on the check cord, substituting a long blast of the whistle for the command "Come here." He will soon learn to respond to either the voice or whistle command.

"Whoa!"

The most important word in the bird-dog trainer's vocabulary is "Whoa!" When the dog has learned that "Whoa" means to stop instantly and remain still, and will obey the command under any and all circumstances, you are well on your way toward having a well-trained dog.

The command should be given only when you mean it, and you should take steps to see that it is obeyed quickly. This will save you many headaches in field training and it will prove of great value when your dog is accompanying you as a companion. Quick use of the command and its instant obedience will prevent the dog from making many mistakes in the field, will be an asset in teaching him to back or honor a pointing dog, will prevent his chasing flushed birds, allow you quickly to change his course in hunting, allow you to stop him as he starts to cross a highway or before he gets into danger, etc. After the dog has learned to whoa promptly at command, remember to use the command sparingly and only when necessary. Don't abuse it, or the dog will soon begin to pay little attention to it.

You can start teaching this command to the puppy at an early age; in fact, as soon as he is weaned. It is best to start at feeding time. The first lesson is simple: Place the feed in front of the puppy. Hold him back from it some four feet or so, restraining him for a while, repeating the command "Whoa." Presently give the command "Go On," and release him, allowing him to rush to his feed. While the command "Whoa" is given, the puppy should be stroked gently. Some trainers use other commands such as "Heed" or "Ter-ho," but "Whoa" is to be preferred. It is short and positive.

This lesson should be repeated at feeding time every day for a week, at least, the puppy being lightly restrained and becoming accustomed to the command. As time goes on, the trainer will find that he can lift the restraint, and the puppy will remain motionless before his feed until the command "Go On" is given. Should he break before ordered, he should be placed into position again and the command repeated.

After a while, place the pan of feed down at a good distance from the puppy. He can then be sent on at the command "Go On" but stopped before he reaches the feed by the sharp command "Whoa." Later the trainer can toss bits of food out and stop the puppy within a few feet of them at command. He will then be under good control, at least, while you are close by.

Take your time in teaching this accomplishment. You want him to learn this lesson thoroughly, and it is a good idea to rehearse him in it throughout his training period and even afterward. Administer no punishment whatever. Restrain the puppy in a kindly manner, and you will find that he will respond to these lessons very readily.

Several of the older writers recommend taking this training a step further. They advocate the employment of two check cords and a post to perfect the dog in this accomplishment. I do not believe in this practice, as I consider it too mechanical and too much needless work. The average amateur will already be prone to put more "Whoa" than "Go" in his dog, and the goal toward which this book directs is the development of a *natural* bird dog, free from mechanical faults. The beginner must always remember that too much curbing, too much restraint, will break the spirit of any dog and frustrate the efforts to make him into a pleasing gunning companion. If the beginner will exercise self-control and practice patience in copious quantities he can, by following the methods outlined in this book, develop his dog into a competent field performer without taking any of the dash or spirit out of him.

After the young dog has learned to obey the command "Whoa" around the yard, your next step is to get him to do it in the field. This will not be so easily accomplished, for there will be much to distract him, and he will want to follow his own inclinations. However, by using the long check cord and stopping him at the command "Whoa," causing him to remain standing for a short while, then rewarding him, you will soon get the desired results.

Next, you can hold your hand in an upraised position when you give the command. He will come to associate the upraised hand with the command, and soon you can stop him by merely holding your hand and arm up. By diligent practice you can stop him at any distance. Don't overdo this, however, as he will begin to look for it and lose some of his independence, and that is a quality you want to preserve.

To Heel

A dog that has been trained to walk directly behind you, or at your side or "at heel" has an accomplishment that will be quite useful in taking him along city streets or through crowded areas. Place the dog on a short lead. Draw him to your side and keep him there by shortening your grip on the lead. Walk along, and as he tries to go in front of you, tap him lightly on the nose with a limber switch and give the command "Heel." Repeat this every time he attempts to pass you and he will soon learn that he must walk at your side or directly behind you when he hears the command "Heel." It is best that he walk at your side, as it will not then be necessary to look around to see where he is. At which side he walks makes no difference, but it is best that he walk on the side opposite to that on which you carry your gun.

Do not be in a hurry to teach your young dog this accomplishment. Wait until he is at least a year old, as very young puppies should be restrained as little as possible. Trips to and from the field may be profitably utilized in teaching your dog to heel.

To Drop

Some trainers teach their young dogs to drop at command, signal, or shot. It is a form of restraint that I do not recommend, except to correct some particular fault, for its importance is minor, and in this practice the danger of taking something out of the dog is again incurred. The value of boldness cannot be minimized.

If, however, you desire to teach your dog to drop, call him to you, place one hand on his shoulders, and force him down, repeating the command "Drop" in a low tone. Hold him in a recumbent position for a time, stroking him the while and repeating the command. Then allow him to regain his feet, romp a bit, and repeat the lesson. He will probably squirm about, roll over and move around, but keep him as still as possible and continue the command.

After he has begun to realize what you want him to do, you may employ mild force by giving him a light cuff occasionally to make him know that he must remain down. When he becomes accustomed to the practice, you may use the whip by laying it on his back lightly at the command "Drop." If he refuses to lie down immediately, repeat the command and tap him with the whip across the shoulders. Soon he will drop immediately at command. These lessons should be given in a quiet room where you will not be disturbed. You may then take him into the yard.

After he will drop at command, cause him to remain in that position while you move away from him. If he attempts to follow or leave his position, bring him back, command him to drop, and keep him down for a time. After he will remain down while you move away from him, you may go further and teach him to drop at some distance from you.

If you care to, you can go still further and teach him to drop at signal. This may be done by raising the right hand each time you give the command "Drop." He will associate the two and after a time drop to either the command or the hand signal. Later on he may be taught to drop to shot in the same manner. Take him slowly in this, and avoid any risk of breaking his spirit. It is not necessary to teach a dog to drop in order to prevent him from jumping up on your person and soiling your clothes with his muddy feet.

This can be accomplished by encouraging him to rear up on you and then trodding lightly upon the toes of his rear feet, giving the command "Down." After a few treatments of this sort no manner of coaxing can cause him to jump up on you.

It should be understood that these lessons can be made part of the dog's everyday life, but that each step should be taken slowly. Don't try to crowd the puppy in his training. Give him plenty of time, confine each lesson to a short period, and obedience to your commands will come to him as a matter of course. All this takes time, but slow progress is worth while, for then you run no risk of affecting the dog's independence or restricting his natural fire and dash. And you will become better acquainted with your dog as you go along.

Chapter 7

STARTING THE YOUNGSTER

๑๛๑

"WHAT is the proper age to start a dog in a course of training?" It is only natural that this is one of the first questions a beginner will ask, and, as many entertain different ideas on the subject, he will no doubt receive a variety of replies.

Again let us remind you that some dogs develop earlier than others. This fact should be constantly borne in mind, for behind it lies the real reason for patience and perseverance in training.

Some sportsmen contend that a puppy's education should be started by the time he is old enough to be taken from his mother. There are, indeed, simple things that can be taught him at that time, but it is generally conceded that this is far too tender an age at which to begin any efforts at serious training.

Of course, we all like to see the pointing instinct assert itself at an early age, for there is nothing prettier than a very young puppy styling up into point on a sparrow, barnyard fowl, or even butterfly. But the ability of a young puppy to absorb training of a serious nature is very limited.

and more harm than good will result from an attempt to overcrowd him.

Many fanciers are of the opinion that a puppy six months of age is old enough to begin to realize what his purpose in life should be, and feel that his experience in the field should start at that time. They hold to the idea that the best way to prevent an aged dog from making mistakes is never to allow him to make them in his earlier career. Hence he will never form bad habits.

There is, indeed, some merit in this argument, yet I do not subscribe to it in its entirety. Nor have I seen a dog that did not make a mistake occasionally. In fact, deliberate mistakes may become agencies of value sometimes. For instance, I know several prominent field-trial handlers who encourage their young dogs to break shot on occasion. It has been their experience that a good fling and a spree of chasing are sometimes very beneficial to a dog that has been crowded in his training, as it has the effect of making him exceedingly keen on his game. College athletic coaches have found that constant drilling causes athletes to go stale, and an occasional indulgence in breaking training sometimes restores the desired edge.

In my opinion, the best time to start a pup's education is after he has passed his first birthday. In the case of many individuals a year and a half or even two years would be better, for the training at that time will be of a more permanent nature.

Of course, there are young dogs that are doing excellent work in the field, hunting intelligently, and handling game properly, before they have reached the age of one year. These, however, are exceptional individuals, but some of them never show any improvement over their puppy form. A puppy that is overcrowded in training and forced to play the part of an all-age dog is very apt to develop into a phlegmatic, methodical performer whose work never approaches brilliancy.

The very young puppy may have a remarkable aptitude for learning simple lessons and tricks when little or no force is employed. He takes to this sort of training in the spirit of playfulness, but when the application of force becomes necessary he is liable to become cowed and his spirit permanently affected. The younger the pupil the greater amount of care must be exercised in his training.

On the other hand, the older dog, provided he has not become too set in his ways, has developed in the natural way, has more self-confidence, and is not so quick to become frightened when mild force is employed. The older dog has the intelligence to better absorb the teachings of the trainer, and his attention is not so easily diverted. He has the desire to do things and this is most essential in the promising pupil. True, he may have his own ideas of how things should be done, but this should not present a serious obstacle, for the bold, self-reliant pupil is the choice of all experienced trainers.

The beginner should not expect too much from his young pupil, for the puppy has not been long in this world and has had very little opportunity to develop his intelligence. The yearling dog is still a neophyte in a world of dogly possibilities, and he might well be compared with a six- or seven-year-old child. The dog may take to his lessons readily, but this is no sure sign that he is possessed of extraordinary intelligence, as he may be doing the things his trainer wants him to do in a spirit of fun only. His progress may be easily deceiving, for he may not be taking his lessons seriously at all. Many a good young dog has been ruined simply because the trainer became too enthusiastic over his apparent mental development and began to expect too much from him.

Some trainers are of the opinion that the young dog should

be fairly well along in his yard-breaking lessons before his field experience begins. I am not in accord with this idea, *for I prefer that the youngster become fully imbued with the desire to hunt before any serious efforts are made to bring him under thorough control. Work in the field best reveals whether or not the prospect is worth while, and there is no need to waste valuable time in yard-breaking if the dog is not endowed with natural qualities. He should, however, be taught to know his name, to come when called, and to feel at ease when placed on a lead or when confined at the end of a chain. These are simple matters that can be taught him in such manner that no danger of his losing any part of his spirit or self-confidence will be incurred.*

If his education in the field is started first, his horizon broadens, he begins to realize that this old world is a pretty big place after all, and that he is a definite part of it. He becomes acquainted with various scents, some of which are exhilarating and even fairly intoxicating. He sees new sights and becomes acquainted with strange surroundings. He discovers that things that are foreign to him at first are only natural parts of the landscape ahead, that they mean him no harm. He learns to chase small birds, insects, and field mice, and all the time he is developing mentally and physically in a natural way. He grows in self-confidence and becomes bold and unafraid. And, above all, his natural instinct to hunt is developing rapidly. It is then that he begins to realize that the trainer plays a part in his daily excursions afield and he will be in a more receptive mood for yard-breaking lessons.

Yard-breaking, unless the tactics employed are administered with great care and patience, almost invariably takes some of the dash and spirit out of the dog. He may regain these qualities after he has had a period in the field and is allowed his head, but if he has learned his lessons too well, or if a considerable amount of force has been exercised in their teaching, he may become so dependent upon his trainer that much encouragement is necessary to interest him in hunting. However, if the desire to hunt is instilled in him before his yard-breaking begins, he will not forget it so readily.

We maintain that yard-breaking *can* be accomplished through such kindly tactics that the dog will hardly realize that he is being forced to do things, or rather in such a way that the pupil is glad to do the things desired of him. But few men possess the patience necessary for the development of the art in such a high degree. So it is only reasonable to assume that the beginner will, on occasion, lose control of his usually calm and unruffled demeanor, especially when his pupil becomes stubborn and sulks.

The first lesson in the field should consist of allowing the young dog to do as he pleases. If he has been brought up in a kennel, almost everything will be strange to him, and care must be taken to prevent him from becoming frightened. He should not be forcibly led up to any object toward which he shows fear, but the trainer should attempt to impart confidence to him and allow him to find out things in a natural way. He should not be allowed to get into mischief or injure himself, however, for a bold puppy is a trusting individual and once his confidence is shattered much damage is done.

Every effort should be made to encourage him to hunt, although no attempts to force him to do so should be countenanced. He may show no inclination to hunt on his first few trips afield, and merely be content to trot along beside you. Do not be too discouraged unless he continues to be disinterested over an extended period in which he is given numerous opportunities. A young field dog possesses an investigating nature, and this should be allowed to develop naturally. The instinct to hunt is highly developed in some dogs at a very early age. Others are slower to start, so the trainer should not become discouraged if his charge shows little interest in finding out things for himself the first time afield. If the puppy is particularly tardy in this respect, an older dog should be taken along a few times and the youngster encouraged by example.

Starting two youngsters together has its advantages and also its drawbacks. Puppies love company and are more satisfied with kennel life if companionship is provided. One puppy can learn a lot from another, and sometimes develop more rapidly if friendly competition is provided. Also a minor quantity of jealousy in their make-ups sometimes spurs them on to learn more rapidly, for often the tardy youngster can be brought around by observing his kennel mate being rewarded with caresses and tidbits for doing something that he has refused to do.

Two puppies are very little more trouble to keep than one, and the value of the companionship often overbalances the extra cost. As each training lesson must be confined to short periods, an extra puppy will require little more of the trainer's time, and it is most interesting to watch the development of a pair, comparing their progress at intervals.

The spirit of competition may become strongly developed in a pair of puppies that are being trained together. While this can be developed into a valuable asset to the trainer if he exercises the proper caution, there is also a danger of its becoming a liability if he allows it full play. The puppies may spring off in a friendly race, and sometimes this gives them a good start toward actual hunting. The trainer should, however, watch carefully to see that they do not become so preoccupied with competitive racing and playing that they forget about everything else. One may be a trifle faster than the other, and the bad habit of trailing is encouraged.

Often a puppy will make prodigious casts in company with another but will show little interest in hunting when taken out alone. Should any signs of this trait become apparent, the youngsters should be separated and taken afield one at a time.

As long as the puppy will hunt, all is going well, for no dog can become a good field performer unless he has the desire in a marked degree. In taking your puppy afield, do not use the same route every time. Change hunting territories frequently, giving him new sections to explore and new sights to see. And do not confine your route to paths and roadways. Take him across country where the going is rough, so that he will become accustomed to negotiating the cover and will not constantly seek the easy footing.

The best way to encourage a young dog to hunt is to hunt yourself. He believes that what you do is the proper thing for him to do. If you adopt an indifferent, careless manner in your trips afield and dodge the difficult cover, he will be inclined to take his cue from your actions. But if, by your manner, you show him that you are seriously interested in the job at hand, he will be more likely to settle to his work in a businesslike way. And this applies not only to field training, but to everything you try to teach him.

Make no attempt to force him to hunt. Encourage him in every way possible, by voice, actions, etc., but let him learn about these things in easy stages. Above all things you want a *natural* bird dog or one that does things because he *wants* to do them. Each new discovery he makes will lead him on to further searchings and, after he has become accustomed to strange surroundings and confident in his ability to take care of himself, his natural desire to hunt will take him afield with a zest.

Allow him his head. Let him chase anything he desires, so long as it does not lead him into trouble. Encourage him in the development of his natural instincts in the natural way, for there will be plenty of time to bring him into hand later. Some may think I am placing too much emphasis on *"natural development"* but if this book does nothing more than convince the beginner that *training* is *not* breaking but is the encouragement, development, and direction of *natural* instincts, I will be satisfied. Too much curbing and crowding will break the dog's spirit and thwart your own desires for a bold dog with complete confidence in himself and his trainer.

Some trainers prefer to farm out a puppy for a definite period before his actual training begins. By this term we mean placing the puppy with a farmer who will allow him to accompany him about his daily agricultural pursuits. This often proves a worth-while practice, as the puppy is brought up in the natural habitat of game, is seldom confined, no attempt is made to curb his natural desires, and his hunting instinct has the opportunity to develop rapidly. A puppy that is allowed the freedom of a farm for a period is generally exceedingly keen to hunt after he has been confined in a kennel for a while, and he is already familiar with conditions in the field when his actual training begins. He has also become acquainted with chickens and other livestock.

This system has its good and bad features and, as is the case in every part of dog training, much depends upon the individual. It might be impractical in most instances and, besides, some puppies when allowed the freedom of open country allow their natural inclinations such full play that they develop into confirmed self-hunters. The desire becomes so firmly imbedded that they are ever afterward hard to control. There is, in every training method, a time to stop, and if the puppy is taken into hand before he becomes too set in his ways, the farming-out process is an excellent practice.

There should be no definite time limit attached to the lessons in the field. If he is content to stroll along with you and is tardy in succumbing to the call of the hunting instinct, it will be well to spend considerable time in your daily jaunts. However, if the pupil shows an aptitude for hunting and goes about his business with a vim, there is a definite time to stop. This is when he shows the first signs of tiring, or even before.

Our desire is to keep the puppy on edge and eager to hunt. The best way to do this is never to allow his thirst for hunting to become sated. Never work him until he becomes thoroughly tired, for then his zest for hunting will be diminished and he will not so eagerly look forward to his next trip afield. Give him a good fling in the field, but never overdo it.

It is most likely that, if he is kept keen for hunting, he will dash away in a happy, carefree manner for a race before he settles to actual hunting. He should be allowed this privilege, for it is a good sign that he is made of real hunting-dog material.

When he shows the first signs of tiring, take him up immediately. Do not allow him to hunt on the way home, but place him on the lead and return him to the kennel. Always lead him or have him walk at heel to and from the field. When he becomes more fully developed and hardened, these periods may be extended. Generally fifteen minutes is long enough at the beginning.

Introduction to the Gun in the Field

After the puppy has become accustomed to trips afield and shows a definite interest in hunting, the gun may be brought into play occasionally. It is assumed that you have adopted the method described in Chapter 3 and, through it, the puppy has come to associate gunfire with feeding time. He now shows no fear of the gun around the kennel, but this is no guarantee that he is immune to gun-shyness, and you must exercise extreme caution in introducing him to the gun in the field.

On one of his regular workouts, take along a lightly loaded small-bore shotgun. After the puppy has had his fling and has settled to hunting in good fashion, wait until he is a good distance from you and chasing a bird of any kind. Then fire the gun one time. The puppy will probably stop hunting and look in your direction. Pay no attention to him but keep walking at your usual pace. If he resumes his cast and continues to hunt, all is well and you may shoot again after a time. Never, however, shoot when the puppy is near you or coming toward you. And never shoot around him until he is chasing.

Should he stop hunting and come to you to see what the noise is about, pay no attention to him but continue your walk. Should he show signs of fear and come to heel, still pay no attention to him but continue to act as if nothing had happened. He will probably regain his courage in a few minutes and resume his hunt. If this occurs, do not shoot around him again that day, but wait until he is in a happier mood. Under no circumstances are you to shoot over him the first time when he is near by.

Do not shoot over the young dog the first time he makes a point. You probably won't have the opportunity anyway, as he will most likely flush the birds and chase them before you can reach them. This is only to be expected, and the puppy should not be punished for it, for such an error, if it is to be so considered, serves to make him more eager to hunt, more anxious to find game, and eradicates any thought that he might become bird-shy.

If, however, you bang away over him on his first point, you run the risk of his becoming frightened by the report of the gun and associating this with the flush of the birds. Consequently, much damage may be done in just this short space of time, as he may become gun-shy and bird-shy. He may also connect this association so strongly that he will leave the next birds he finds, and develop the habit of blinking, a fault exceedingly hard to correct. Blinking is when a dog finds birds but leaves them without pointing, or points them and leaves them before his master arrives to flush. This is generally a man-made fault and is brought about when the dog comes to associate birds with punishment of some sort. He has not lost his desire to hunt but he fears birds or the consequences of pointing or flushing them. Not all blinkers are gun-shy nor are all gun-shy dogs blinkers.

The champion pointer, So Big, campaigned so successfully by the dean of professional trainers, the late James M. Avent, was almost ruined by gun-handling carelessness. As a puppy, So Big was an outstanding individual. He won several of the largest puppy stakes of the season and showed great promise. Near the end of the season he was returned to his owner, at the owner's request, for competition in an amateur stake. In a workout, in which his owner had several of his admiring friends along, So Big pointed a covey of quail stanchly, standing up in grand style. Several members of the group, forgetful or unmindful of the fact that the puppy had never been shot over on point, blazed away when the covey was flushed, frightening the young dog out of his wits. For a long time after that So Big was gun-shy, and would have been just another worthless bird dog had he not had the care, attention, and patient training afforded by that master, the sage of Hickory Valley, Tennessee.

Even during his sensational all-age career, when the dog appeared in the winner's circle many times, he always seemed to associate the rise of birds with gunfire and on many occasions he flattened out in the cover when he pointed. Even such an excellent trainer as Jim Avent could not entirely eradicate the unfortunate experience from So Big's memory.

Training and shooting, as the amateur knows them, do not go well together. The trainer must forgo the pleasure of shooting for a time if he is to accomplish the most good. Opportunities for good shots will naturally be fewer over a young dog than over a finished performer, and if the trainer shoots every time a bird flushes, little will be accomplished.

Killing birds over the young dog is most essential to his training, but these birds must be shot over *his points,* and not when he purposely or accidentally flushes. Shooting birds that the dog has flushed encourages him to remain unsteady and interferes with the progress of his training.

Chapter 8

THE POINTING INSTINCT AND
HOW TO DEVELOP IT

❦

ESSENTIAL to the complement of a good gun dog is a well-defined, strongly developed pointing instinct. In some individuals this instinct asserts itself at an earlier age than in others, and those in which it is latent must be encouraged to point every time the opportunity presents itself.

The pointing instinct has always been the subject of much discussion. Some sportsmen contend that it is a natural development that accompanied the transition of the dog from the wild to the domestic state, for in the wild he was forced to stalk his game for food. They hold that the immobile pause that now characterizes a point is the result of the development of the crouch that preceded the wild dog's spring upon his prey.

Others aver that, originally, this quality was not an instinct at all, but a product of the trainer's art, which, after constant employment through generation after generation, has evolved into a definite instinct characteristic of the bird-dog breeds.

When dogs were first taught to "set" or "sit" or, as we

now term it, "point" is unknown. Anthony Wood's *Athenæ Oxonienses* (1721) credits Robert Dudley, son of Robert Dudley, Earl of Leicester, born in 1574, with being the first exponent of the sport of bird-dog training. The following passage, referring to Dudley, is quoted: "He was a handsome, personable Man, tall of Stature, red hair'd, and of admirable comport, and above all, noted for riding the great Horse, for tilting, and for his being the first of all that taught a Dog to sit in order to catch partridges."

This, however, is more than likely an erroneous statement, as in *The Master of Game,* written between the years 1406 and 1413, Edward, second Duke of York, had the following to say concerning the spaniel: ". . . for their kind cometh from Spain, notwithstanding there are many in other countries . . . but their craft is of the partridge and the quail . . . and when they be taught to be couchers [to set] they be good to take partridges and quail with a net."

Dogs were known to point game many years even before this era, as the following example given by Xenophon (434-355 B.C.), a friend of Socrates, denotes: "Some again go a long way around in the first instance and anticipating the trail in their circuit before they have reached it, pass the hare by, and when they do sight the hare in advance, tremble, and do not proceed until they see him make a move."

We know that in the olden days, when the net was employed in bagging game birds, the dog was taught to crouch or drop on point. This was necessary in order that the net might be drawn over him and the birds at the same time. However, after the use of the gun as a sporting accessory became more general, the net was discarded and the dog taught to stand his game. Thus he was more easily found in high cover.

Whatever the origin of this quality, it is now recognized as a definite instinct, in which but few pointers and setters are lacking. It is, however, necessary that this instinct be properly developed. Some dogs are overanxious to point, and if allowed and encouraged to exercise this impulse too freely, will develop the habit of false pointing, thereby giving no end of disappointment to the hunter. In others the instinct is not so strong and causes them to pause only momentarily, establishing what is called a flash point, which in reality is but a short pause before flushing the birds.

Thus the beginner, in developing the pointing instinct to the degree of stanchness, must take care not to overdo his work and develop his prospect into a false pointer.

If at an early age the young dog responds to the urge by pointing sparrows, barnyard fowl, pigeons, or even butterflies and other insects, all well and good, for the sooner he demonstrates this quality the better. However, if the instinct appears to be latent it is well to encourage it by artificial methods. Naturally, it is best to get the young dog to pointing first in the field. There he learns to point game and game only. But, more likely than not, this may be impractical, and much can be done in the yard to encourage the pointing instinct. This should be practiced only when the puppy is very young, three to five months old. After that he becomes bored.

Sight Pointing

One method, almost sure to produce results, is employed in the teaching of sight pointing. This practice does not generally afford the added exhilaration that accompanies the scent of game birds, but it is of value in establishing the habit patterns of pointing. By this method the puppy accustoms himself to muscular rigidity, mental tenseness, and impulse control.

Attach a stout string, three or four feet in length, to the small end of a fishing pole. To the end of the string attach a freshly killed English sparrow, which will give off some scent, or a piece of paper or cloth, which will attract the puppy's attention. Secure his interest by twitching the object slowly across the lawn in front of him.

He will most probably begin to stalk it and attempt to pounce upon it. Prevent his doing so by snatching the object out of his reach. After a few attempts to catch it, he will begin to stiffen up into a point when the object is allowed to remain stationary. Should he begin to relax, a light jerk on the pole will cause the object to move slightly, and this is generally sufficient to cause him to resume his tense attitude. It will do no harm to allow him to catch the object occasionally. This will serve to whet his interest.

Should he show no inclination to point, and merely demonstrate a desire to catch the object, allow him to chase it for a considerable time, keeping it out of his reach until he has grown somewhat tired. He will most likely welcome the rest, yet retain his interest in the object, which generally results in a point.

After he begins to point, have an assistant handle the pole, and when the youngster is pointing stanchly and rigidly put your hands on him, gently stroking him along the back, and cautioning him with the repetition of the word "Whoa" in a low tone. He will begin to associate this word with the establishment of a point, and it will serve the trainer well in future lessons.

If the puppy still shows no inclination to point or even stalk the object, fasten a cord to his collar, allow him to chase the object for a while and, bringing it to rest, restrain him from catching it by grasping the cord. Stroke the puppy along the back, twitching the object in front of him but restraining him with the cord the while; use the word "Whoa" in a low tone occasionally, and you will find that in a short time he will point the object stanchly for considerable periods at a time. He will enter into this procedure with enthusiasm and will begin to enjoy the function of pointing.

The trainer should not take this practice too seriously, for while it has some value, it is relatively unimportant. It will serve to amuse both the owner and the puppy, however, and can do no harm unless indulged in too frequently. Five or six minutes at a time is sufficient. The puppy's interest may wane in longer periods. This method can be used effectively when the puppy is of tender age, but should be discontinued when he becomes old enough to start field work.

Pointing Game

The trainer is more practically concerned with the evidence of the pointing instinct in the field. In developing the pointing instinct to the degree of stanchness, there is the danger of the dog's acquiring a number of faults that may be difficult to correct in later training.

If the puppy does not establish a definite point the first time he comes in contact with game, do not become discouraged. If he establishes any semblance of a point, some progress is made. Of course, it is best if the dog does not flush and chase the first birds he points, but such an error is only to be expected. The scent of his first covey of birds is fairly intoxicating; it practically paralyzes him into a momentary point, and then there comes rushing into his brain the mad desire to dash into the birds and chase them. Seldom can he resist this temptation, and the trainer should not worry if he succumbs, for this is an indication of boldness and breeds for self-confidence. He will soon learn that he cannot catch them and will very probably begin to point of his own accord. As long as he shows the desire to hunt, demonstrates that he has a good nose, can find birds, and is not afraid to flush them, you can rest assured that he is made of the right material.

If, after several months of field experience, he continues to flush and chase his birds and shows no inclination to point them, it is then time to take a hand in the development of his pointing instinct and the curbing of his desire to flush.

Locate a covey of birds in a likely place. Attach a long check cord to the dog's collar, and work him toward the covey's range, taking advantage of the wind and the time of day. Your task now is to get your hands on the cord as soon as the dog shows signs of scenting the covey. In this manner you can bring him to a stop before he flushes the birds. Then go to him quickly, for once you have your hands on him, much can be accomplished toward teaching him a lesson in stanchness.

Stroke the dog along the back, repeating the word "Whoa" in a low tone. If he shows no signs of stiffening up into a definite point, it is possible that the birds are a considerable distance from him, and it will be well to allow him to approach closer to them. This can be done by having him walk slowly by your side, while you caution him in a quiet manner, using the command "Whoa." When he shows unmistakable signs of being close to the birds, check him once more, again stroking him along the back and repeating the command.

This time he will most likely respond by becoming rigid in a well-established point. This is the situation the trainer has been wishing for, and he should make the most of it. With one hand on the dog's collar to prevent him from breaking, stroke him with the other hand from his shoulders to the tip of his tail, raising the tail well above the level of the back.

Presently grasp the dog by the root of the tail, raise him slowly and gently off his hind feet, and place him in position again. Repeat this several times, all the while using the command "Whoa" in a low tone. Finally, still keeping one hand on him to prevent his breaking, shove him forward steadily, but gently, putting the pressure on his haunches. Care should be excercized not to shove the dog out of his tracks, as the purpose of this pressure is to cause him to resist it by setting back against it. When he shows this inclination, you have accomplished much toward bringing him to a degree of stanchness.

Do not go too far with him on the first lesson, but handle him gently for a while, particularly if he takes kindly to the handling and appears to enjoy it. Then step forward and flush the birds. The dog will probably break and chase. If he is of a timid disposition or is lacking in range, it will be well to allow him to do so for a few times, for his chasing will have the tendency to make him bolder and encourage him to range out wider.

If he is a bold, independent, and headstrong dog, it will be best to try to keep him from breaking, if you can do so without applying force or frightening him in any way. The manner in which he is handled on the flush of his first birds will have a definite bearing upon his actions on game in the future, and the trainer should take every precaution to prevent his associating his first point with any element that might be distasteful to him.

If you can get your hands on him before he breaks, all well and good, for then you may stroke him and reassure him while restraining him. But if he breaks past you and chases the birds, do not try to check him by loud yells, dashing after him, or jerking the check cord. These tactics may frighten him severely, so much so that he might associate them with the flush of his first birds, thereby acquiring a fear of game.

Let him go, and when the chase is well under way, fire the gun. Continue this for several days, and after you are certain that he has no fear of the gun, try to kill a bird over every point he makes, provided, of course, that he allows you to flush the bird. Nothing encourages a young dog to hunt or to point more than killing birds for him, but you should never shoot at birds he deliberately, or accidentally, flushes. Show him that "no stay" means "no pay," and you will be developing stanchness.

The importance of handling the dog on point cannot be overlooked, for most dogs love this practice and look forward to it in connection with a point. Kind, gentle handling on point imparts confidence. It relieves him of the uneasiness that seems to come to some with the scent of game birds, gives him the feeling that he is pleasing you, and encourages stanchness. And stanchness in a high degree is the *desideratum*.

As you continue to get your dog on point, you may begin gradually to take liberties with him, but handling him more and in a somewhat rougher manner. Stroke the tense dog gently as usual. Pick him up by the tail and drop him several times. Shove him gently forward, allowing him to settle back. Change his position by turning his body in an angle. He may be lifted completely off the ground and dropped back into position. Sometimes he may be turned completely around, and then will point over his shoulder. All this is pleasing to the dog and he will look forward to it.

After he has proved his stanchness under these conditions the trainer may go a step further by picking him up bodily and tossing him a step or two forward. He will invariably strike the ground pointing if he has been handled right in the beginning. The trainer may go so far as to pitch him right into the birds, but this is pure show-off and is not recommended to the novice.

This handling comes to be associated with the point. The dog looks forward to the approach of his trainer, and instead of becoming uneasy he instinctively sets himself to receive the stroking and handling that he enjoys. This practice may be discontinued after the dog becomes stanch on point; yet it will do no harm to engage in it occasionally whenever it is considered desirable.

Approaching the Point

Some dogs become nervous upon the approach of the handler. They become so affected by this nervousness that flushes frequently occur. This can be corrected by adopting the proper method of approach. At first, go to your dog from the side, and if possible walk toward him in a quartering direction. He thus becomes aware of your movements and is not upset by noise behind him: It is well to stop occasionally and caution him with the low word "Whoa." Finally move up to the dog, place your hand on him and stroke him as usual. Raise him up by the tail, drop him and shove gently against his haunches. After the dog has become accustomed to this method of approach, vary it by first coming to him from the side, stroking him as usual; then walk away to the rear, making sufficient noise to inform him of your movements. Approach him again, cautioning him occasionally with the word "Whoa" and pausing at intervals.

After several similar occurrences, approach him from the rear, always allowing him to hear you. Handle him as usual. Then approach him from different directions, until he is caused no uneasiness no matter from what direction you appear. It is then well to get him accustomed to a noisy approach. Loud talking, singing, and even whistling may be indulged in, and, after a while, the dog may be approached in a run. But always upon going to him, fondle him with gentle stroking.

Stanchness

Some dogs are thoroughly stanch when their trainers are near, but they cannot be depended upon to remain long on point when the handler is missing. Stanchness in the highest degree has been developed when the dog will remain on point for an interminable length of time, and notable examples of this have been recorded. Colonel Thornton's famous pointers, Juno and Pluto, are said to have remained motionless on point for an hour and a quarter, while they were being sketched by the celebrated artist Gilpin.

One way to encourage such stanchness is to get the dog thoroughly settled on point and then walk away from him to the rear, sit down in some place within calling distance but out of his sight, and then watch him. He may begin to show signs of uneasiness or unrest after a while. It is then that you should caution him and let him know you are watching him, but remain out of sight. He may become leg weary after a time and lie down on his point. It will be well then to go to him, raise him up, stroke him a few times, and flush his birds.

If the birds have run away from him, encourage him to relocate them and then put them up for him without delay. A few occurrences like this and he will begin to realize that you will eventually find him if he becomes lost on point, and hence will remain stanch for a surprisingly long time.

I know of any number of occasions, in field trials, when contending dogs would disappear to be found many minutes afterward, tucked away on point in some little ravine or gulley, having remained stanch all the while even though the gallery, the handler, and a couple of scouts had ridden within a few feet of them several times.

Sometimes individuals are found that like to hunt, show intelligence in searching, have good noses, but do not seem to manifest the pointing instinct. A dog of this type should be led in behind a pointing dog and encouraged to point by example.

Attach a short lead to his collar and lead him up to within plain sight of the pointing dog. Stop him, and employ the stroking method, as outlined above, using the command "Whoa" in a low tone. If he shows no interest in the pointing dog, bring him up closer, taking advantage of the wind in your approach so that he will get the scent. It may be necessary to take him up alongside the pointing dog, but a few lessons of this nature will give him the idea.

This dog should be given as much work on game as possible and afforded every opportunity to point. If he continues to show no inclination to point and is indifferent to the pointing dog, it is best to dispose of him as not worth the effort to bring him around.

False Pointing

Some dogs indulge the pointing instinct to such a degree that is becomes a fault. These individuals are known as false pointers and make many points that produce no game. Such a dog may possess a hypersensitive nose or be of such a timid nature that he brings this instinct into play whenever he feels the slightest urge.

False pointing may also be caused by the continual cautioning or hacking of his trainer, so care must be taken to develop the pointing instinct naturally. This fault is corrected by working the dog alone and paying little attention to his points for a time. Frequently false pointers pay too much attention to their brace mates in the hope of obtaining an opportunity to back. By working him alone, the temptation of watching his brace mate is removed.

If the trainer has studied his dog he can generally tell when the dog is pointing game and when he is not quite sure of himself. So when he styles up into point, assure yourself that it is a "ghost point" and then order the dog on, either with whistle or voice. If he remains stanch, go on your way and pay no attention to him. Presently he will feather a bit, make a short cast or two, and then go on ahead. The indifference treatment is the best way to cure the fault of false pointing.

Do not, however, be ready to condemn a dog for false pointing until he continually commits these errors, for sometimes you cannot tell but what his birds have recently flushed when you were not in sight. For instance, when I was one of the judges in the National Championship of 1933, the pointers Schoolfield and Bailey's Proctor Mike were down together. Mike made a short cast to the side and rear. As we rounded a bend in the course, a covey of quail flushed wild directly ahead. In less than a minute Mike swung through, caught the ground scent, and flashed into a stylish point. The birds were gone, of course, but the dog was not charged with a false point.

Pottering on Foot Scent

Some dogs are inclined to potter on foot scent. This should not be tolerated, and immediate steps should be taken to discourage this fault as soon as it becomes apparent. This is best done by forcing the dog on when he shows the desire to linger or dwell on a foot scent. If he desires to follow the foot scent, all right, provided he does it with a high head and at a good pace. The dog that prowls or potters along on foot scent is more apt to flush the birds than the one that approaches his birds at a gallop and with his head held high. The low-headed, pottering dog is apt to become so interested in ferreting out the foot scent that he will come too close to the birds before he recognizes the body scent. Crowd him every time he shows signs of pottering. This may result in an occasional flush, but it will teach the dog to approach his game without hesitation.

It is not everyone who has ready access to good game country. Sometimes it is well nigh impossible to secure enough bird work to train a dog properly under natural conditions. It is then that the trainer can resort to the use of hand-reared game birds, guinea fowl, or even pigeons. We deal with this subject in another chapter.

Chapter 9

RANGING, TURNING TO WHISTLE, QUARTERING

⚘

A DOG'S range may be defined as the distance he will hunt from his handler. Some young dogs are more independent than others and will naturally adopt a wide range. Such ambitious running may be entirely unsuitable for the type of country you hunt in or the kind of game bird to be gunned, so the youngster's range must be restricted to fit the occasion. On the other hand, some dogs range in too close to the handler, and it may become necessary to give them considerable encouragement in order to cause them to accustom themselves to making wider casts.

Quail, pheasants, grouse, and woodcock are the four most important upland game birds in this country that are hunted with bird dogs. None of the habits of these birds is entirely similar, and their various habitats differ materially in the matter of terrain.

Consequently the dog that is hunted on quail alone must work his country in a different manner from that employed by the dog that is hunted exclusively on grouse and woodcock. Grouse and woodcock are generally found in the same type of territory, and so the good grouse dog is more often than not a good woodcock dog. This doesn't work both ways, however, for grouse are much harder to handle than woodcock.

In the matter of range, a good quail dog compares favorably with a good pheasant dog, but the habits of the two birds differ considerably and the seasoned quail dog handles his country in a somewhat different manner than his brother who works on the wily pheasant. Some dogs have the ability to adapt their range to different types of country and handle themselves properly no matter what type of terrain they are asked to work. But this quality is unusual and valuable, indeed, when a dog possesses it in a marked degree.

The best quail-covey dog can be depended upon to swing out wide, but the dog of extreme range can seldom be brought in to work on singles satisfactorily. It often requires constant hacking or calling him in to make him restrict his range and hunt out a narrow area, as is required in hunting single quail. On the other hand, the best singles dog adopts a more moderate range all the time and hence cannot vie with the wider dog in finding coveys. So it will be well not to expect too much of one dog.

The beginner will know what type of game bird is native to his locality. Observe the methods of ground work employed by the best local dogs and then try to have your pupil conform his range to this ideal.

The good quail dog learns to hunt wide, working out the birdy places on both sides of the area to be hunted, skimming the edges and wood slots, and passing up what is obviously barren ground.

The pheasant dog works his country a little closer, taking in all the lowlands, swinging along the fence rows, and quartering through the corn and grainfields.

The grouse and woodcock dog is still more thorough in

his ground work, quartering the cover to maintain contact with his handler at all times, working the terrain thoroughly, and missing no opportunity to investigate corners and nooks that may afford refuge to the artful ruffed grouse.

There are definite reasons for these dogs using different methods of ground work. Through experience, which is the best teacher, they have learned how to work the terrain typical of their sections to the best advantage and with the least effort. The quail dog learns to know the habits of Bob White's family. Mister Bob spends little time in barren cotton fields and marshy meadows, but likes to feed along the edges of thick places so that he will have instant access to cover. He works along ditch banks, for here feed is to be found and he can feast in comparative safety. The good quail dog comes to realize this and consequently conforms his ground work to these habits. The quail dog that has had several seasons of proper experience learns to change his methods of hunting with the time of the day, working closer in the cover during the middle of the day, and ranging out in the open in the afternoon.

The pheasant dog comes to know that old Ring Neck likes the swampy, marshy places and works out each of these areas thoroughly. He also discovers that cornfields are favorite places for these birds. He learns that the pheasant does not "lay" as well as quail, so he approaches it in a somewhat different manner. And he acquires most of this knowledge through experience, although the trainer can aid him in gaining it. He must approach his quarry in a fast, snappy fashion, which very often forces the bird to lay. Any extremely cautious approach is generally a waste of time, as the pheasant is a runner and more times than not will sneak away from a pointing dog.

The grouse and woodcock, or cover, dog is the fellow that has particular need for "numbers in his head." The ruffed grouse is the wariest of the species hunted by bird dogs, the wisest, and the hardest to handle. He is generally a lone ranger, although you will often flush more than one from the same spot. Each representative of this breed is an individual in himself, smart and unpredictable. Just when you think you have outguessed him, he will do the exact opposite and frustrate your plans. The man who owns a really good grouse dog owns an animal that is almost beyond price. There are any number of dogs that will hunt well, point grouse stanchly, and give their masters a fair amount of shooting. But this doesn't make them really good grouse dogs. Most good grouse dogs win their laurels through experience, and seldom it is that a grouse dog reaches the peak of his form under five years. There are some dogs, however, that seem to catch on quickly to the knack of handling grouse, grouse covers, and country properly at a comparatively early age.

I have the pleasure of being one of the trio of judges that crowned the pointer, The Texas Traveler, owned by Dr. A. L. Ziliak, Bay City, Mich., Grand National Grouse Champion for 1947. The Texas Traveler, a worthy son of the several-times field-trial champion The Texas Ranger was only a few days over three years old when he won his coveted crown. But the Traveler is one of those unusual dogs that stand out in any company, and his performance on that occasion was nothing short of brilliant. Incidentally, proof of his versatility lies in the fact that he has been hunted on grouse, woodcock, pheasants, and quail from Michigan to Florida, giving a good account of himself on all species and in all sections.

The ruffed grouse (partridge) spends most of his time in heavy cover, just where you can never tell but certain little pockets and corners are always inviting. So are old abandoned apple orchards along heavily wooded areas. White pines, alders, poplar, and junipers make good grouse covers, and he is to be found along old cart roads and ditches in heavy woods. You have to look for him where you find him, which makes the grouse dog's job all the harder. However, grouse do have certain areas or covers that they seem to prefer and one or more of these "pats" is generally to be found in them in season, no matter if you have already taken several out of them.

The grouse dog soon learns that, as he is to hunt in heavy or thick cover, he must restrict his range and quarter his country if he is to maintain contact with his handler and be of most service to the gun. He soon finds out that grouse are particularly wild and generally must be approached with caution or exceptional dash if an involuntary flush is to be avoided. Some dogs have the knack of slamming into their points almost on top of their quarry, literally mesmerizing the game into laying. Others seem to sense just how close they can come without flushing the bird and handle themselves accordingly.

The reader may wonder why I say that a really *top* performer on grouse must possess a greater variety of good qualities than any other American gun dog. During the running of the 1947 Grand National Grouse Championship, the board of directors of that organization asked Clarke Venable and me to write, in as few words as possible without sacrificing essentials, our description of the ideal grouse dog. We submitted the following, which was unanimously adopted as the standard for the Grand National Grouse Championship:

The ideal grouse dog is the one we seek; he is never attained. He escapes us because in his development we ourselves develop; he is never found because we grow more rigid in our requirements, more capable of sounder interpretations of true values. But our search for the ideal is guided by four basic qualities that are requisite.

Henry P. Davis shooting over Beau Courageous, famous setter owned by Harold S. Garman

The great pointer, Ariel, winner of the National Free-for-All Championship and three times National Champion, owned by A. G. C. Sage

The English setter Elcova Jazz, a superb gun dog owned by Elias C. Vail

The stylish Irish setter, Rufus McTybe O'Cloisters, owned by Edwin M. Berolzheimer

Allamuchy Valley Joe, splendid Brittany Spaniel owned by Alan R.
Stuyvesant   © *Percy T. Jones*

German Shorthaired pointers: Major Berg's Choice (pointing),
owned by George McNee, and Ace von Schwarenberg (backing),
owned by Glen W. Nordvall

Puppies sight pointing artificial game

Ten-week-old puppies pointing guinea fowl

Setter puppy, Mississippi Zenith, at nine weeks of age pointing live quail

A perfectly broken shooting dog, field-trial-winning pointer bitch, Hannah Dustin, owned by the author and trained by his methods

Ideal points on a divided find

The judges in the 1936 National Bird Dog Championship: left to right — Henry P. Davis, the late Hobart
Ames, and Nash Buckingham

Ideal backing! Ghost's Eugene backed by Pastime King, Phil
Essig, Hawk's Spectre, and Eugene's Ghost

A group of famous bird dogs: Champion Kirk's Lucky Light backed by Kirk's Wonder Boy, Kirk's Siasconset, Kirk's Ashantee Dominant, and Kirk's Master's Boy, owned by Harry D. Kirkover

Great field-trial champions and gun dogs as well: (left) Champion Hillbright Susannah, owned by M. G. Dudley, (right) Champion Tarheelia's Lucky Strike, owned by Gerald M. Livingston

A group of professional bird-dog trainers at the Pointer Club of
America trials, 1931   © *John G. Hemmer*

The portable quail call-back trap

If the dog be lacking in any one of them he is far removed from the ideal; but when he possesses them to their fullest he is a workman worthy of highest praise. Briefly, these qualities are:

(1) NOSE (2) INTELLIGENCE (3) CONFORMATION (4) HEART

(1) He must possess that superior quality of nose that leads him unerringly and swiftly to his quarry. There will be no pottering, no time-killing rechecking, no low carriage of the head, no rooting for scent, and no slouchy carriage that speaks of uncertainty. If the nose be truly superior, it will be equal to his pace, however swift. It will tell him with faultless accuracy the precise location of his game. This is the first requirement.

(2) Given such a nose, the ideal grouse dog must then have the high intelligence to apply what he has learned in the field of experience and willingly and gladly convert that knowledge to the advantage of his owner. The ideal grouse dog has learned that his search must be conducted quietly; that his natural quarry is both wise and wary; that the game sought has certain rather fixed habits and characteristics—which are well known to the dog of superior intelligence. Such a dog wastes no time in nonbirdy places. Natural objectives become second nature to him. He reaches for them without undue direction on the part of his handler because his intelligence is supported by a factor never within the capacity of the handler—namely, that superior nose. The two qualities are not only necessary one to the other, but are actually inseparable.

(3) The third requisite is conformation. On this volumes have been written, but it can be dismissed with a sentence: Conformation is nothing but *soundness,* and that which is *sound* has great beauty, great utility, and easy grace. Without soundness the nose and intelligence will fail in the test; with it, the sound body can, with tireless energy, carry that intelligence and nose to the point of impact with game. Such contact is the goal of the quest, and if that fails, all fails.

(4) The fourth necessary attribute is heart. If that be lacking, all the other attributes will fail to lift the dog to the pinnacle of perfection. But given the stout heart that carries merrily and eagerly on and on when every muscle and sinew cries for rest; that never quits or bends away from the roughest going,

then you have the true foundation for the other necessary attributes.

Such are the four priceless and always present qualities of the ideal grouse dog!

The cover dog of experience recognizes native woodcock covers, i.e., low, wet alder runs in which these timber doodles like to bore. He discovers that he can take far more chances with these birds than he can with grouse and approaches them accordingly. He also learns that sun-streaked hill slopes with marshy spots and damp places produce woodcock on pleasant afternoons. He overlooks no low or damp covers where woodcock feed, either as natives or on their southward migrations. His pace is generally necessarily moderate and his range restricted, but his style and carriage should be merry and lofty.

Ranging for Quail and Pheasants

If you are to develop your puppy for use on pheasants or quail, start his field work in open country. Select an area that is fairly level in order that he may be able to see you at considerable distances. It should not be devoid of cover entirely but should contain several birdy-looking places and afford several turns. This is to eliminate the danger of encouraging the habit of straight-line running.

At first, walk down the middle of the area, encouraging the puppy to range out as wide as possible. Allow him his head and let him hunt any part of the area he desires. If he gets behind, blow the whistle long blasts to attract his attention and keep walking at a brisk pace. He will soon learn that you want him to keep in front of you and that he must work at good speed in order to do so.

Work him over the same ground for a couple of weeks, or

until he knows it so well that he will cover the entire area without depending upon you for guidance. Walk over the course or area at good pace and never allow him to loaf or potter. Keep him moving at good speed. After he comes to know the course thoroughly he will begin to stretch out and take in additional territory. Make no effort to direct him for a time, but if he should disappear from sight for a little while blow long blasts on the whistle in order that he might locate you. Don't become too concerned about him if he doesn't show up right away. Just keep on blowing the whistle and go to some prominence where you can see him or he can see you. If he persists in staying away, however, go after him.

After he has gained confidence in himself and lost his fear of losing you, change hunting territories frequently, taking him into strange country. When he disappears from sight it is well to quicken your pace and go to the highest point on the course so that he may see you as soon as possible. If he can locate you quickly he will be less apt to cut back to find you, and the sight of you will encourage him to continue his hunting at good range.

To further increase his range, work him from horseback. This will enable you to travel faster and see him at greater distances. It will force him to quicken his pace and allow him to locate you easily when he is far away. It will also eliminate delay in getting to him when he is on point.

Always blow two short blasts of the whistle when you cast him off. He will begin to interpret this as a signal to go out and will learn to swing out on a wider cast whenever he hears the two short blasts. Whenever he starts to come back to you, trot toward him with upraised hand, giving two short blasts of the whistle at frequent intervals. This will serve to teach him that this signal means for him to widen his casts. After a while he will respond to it mechanically, turning out whenever the signal is given.

Take him up before he begins to tire, and in doing so always blow one long blast of the whistle at well-spaced intervals and stand in your tracks. Call to him and encourage him to come straight to you, petting him when he obeys. Never go to him unless necessary.

Quartering

After the puppy has developed considerable range, he may be prone to work only on one side of the area, for he wants to keep in touch with you and fears that he may get behind if he tries to take in too much territory. Now is the time to teach him to quarter. Quartering is not so essential in the education of the quail dog as it is in the schooling of one that is to be used on pheasants exclusively, but it is an accomplishment that will prove of value in hunting any game bird.

Start the puppy out as usual. Allow him to swing to one side of the course. Reduce your own pace slightly. When he has completed his first cast, or worked to the end of a birdy spot, blow a long blast of the whistle to attract his attention and walk in a quartering direction toward the other side of the course. Be sure that he sees that you are changing direction, wave to him as he is looking toward you, and if he does not respond immediately, walk slowly, blowing long blasts at frequent intervals. He will soon realize that you do not intend to follow him and will most likely swing out in front of you in the direction you are going.

Never attempt to break his casts as long as he is working in likely looking cover or is heading toward good bird ground. Always have an objective toward which to send him. After he is definitely turned in the proper direction, change your own course and walk straight forward. When he has completed this cast, again attract his attention with the whistle, turn toward the other side of the area, and wave him in that direction.

After you have worked him in this fashion for a time, he will learn that you want him to work both sides of the hunting section and will readily respond to the whistle and the wave of the hand. At first, in turning him, always start walking in the direction you want him to go. This encourages him to quarter the country. After a time the whistle and a wave of the hand will be all that is necessary to send him across the section. If you adopt a slower pace it will allow him to cover both sides of the area and still keep in front of you.

Bear in mind that these lessons will require time and that you cannot expect immediate results. And never try to turn the puppy when he is making an intelligent cast toward likely country.

Turning to Whistle

Most dogs will naturally turn to the whistle. This seems to be instinctive with them. If, however, the puppy is obstinate and continues to ignore the long blast of the whistle, attach the check cord to him. Blow long light blasts of the whistle and with each blast jerk him toward you. Repeat this several times and then release him and resume hunting. If he continues to refuse to respond, attach the check cord again. Blow the whistle, jerk him with every blast, and apply the whip lightly. He will soon become convinced that one blast of the whistle is associated with restraint. This is not recommended for timid dogs or dogs not well advanced in training. Too much whip is never good and in this connection may make the puppy whistle-shy.

The good pheasant dog will quarter through high cover

and damp slashes, working these sections out thoroughly, and he will also work corn and grainfields in a similar manner. Hence it is essential that he be given much work in country of this nature. Never let the pheasant dog potter on foot scent. These birds are known for their running proclivities, and the dog that roads up slowly and puzzles about on foot scent will find himself literally left at the post. When your dog shows signs of making game, see that he keeps moving at a good pace, even at the risk of a flush, for the bird is more liable to run away from him than it is to lay to his point. Many a disappointed gunner has walked a considerable distance to a pointing dog only to see Old Ringneck sail away, out of gun range, after having run away from the dog. The experienced pheasant dog learns to approach his game in a fast, snappy manner, establishing a decisive point. He has intelligence enough to realize when the bird is running away from him and will break his point, roading up to pin the bird again. Often the dog will circle the running bird, and stop him by pointing him from the opposite side.

Work the young dog in good game country whenever possible. Give him as much experience in bird finding as you can. He will then recognize likely looking country, learn the ranging habits of game birds, and waste little time in hunting out sections that are obviously barren.

The Grouse Dog's Range

While the quail and pheasant hunter can stroll along, allowing his dog to swing out over the country at good range, the successful grouse hunter must employ different tactics. Ruffed grouse (partridge) are exceedingly wild and possessed of an extraordinarily keen sense of self-preservation. The pheasant and quail hunter generally knows when his game will flush and in about what direction it will fly. The grouse hunter, on the other hand, must be ever on the alert, for most of his chances are snap shots and, in good grouse country, he seldom knows when to expect them.

In good pheasant and quail country there are always certain spots that are seldom frequented by game. In good grouse covers any part of the area may be productive. For that reason it is highly important that the grouse dog quarter his cover thoroughly and maintain constant contact with his master. Most grouse hunting is done in thick cover and, in order to maintain that necessary contact, the grouse dog must adopt a moderate range.

These birds are particularly wary and nothing frightens them more than the human voice. Hence, the grouse hunter cannot be constantly directing his dog by the use of his voice. Only a few yells are sufficient to put every grouse within hearing distance on the move, and so it is easily seen that the grouse dog must be especially tractable. A low whistle and a wave of the hand should be all that is necessary to turn him.

This tractability may be induced by an intensive course of yard breaking, but herein lies the danger of turning the dog into a slow, pottering, mechanical performer, dependent upon his owner's signals for hunting instructions. Yard breaking is all right in its proper sphere, but the average amateur is quite apt to overdo it. Consequently the making of an excellent grouse dog is a slow process and one that requires careful procedure and infinite patience. Work, and plenty of it, is the best agency through which it can be accomplished.

Select a narrow strip of heavily wooded country, bordered on each side by open fields. Start the puppy in at one end. He is quite apt to cast to the side immediately and dash out into the open. Call him back each time he goes out of the cover, and remain in the heavy vegetation yourself. Work the cover in a zigzag fashion, always checking him when he nears the open. He will soon learn to restrict his casts to the confines of the cover.

If the puppy is particularly levelheaded, and he should be if he is to make an excellent grouse dog, it might be best to teach him to quarter before giving him much work in the cover. This can be accomplished by working him in the same manner as recommended for the quail and pheasant dog, but conducting his lessons in much smaller fields.

When working him in the cover, he *must* learn to hunt *for* you. The good grouse dog should remain in sight most of the time, and prolonged absences should be prima-facie evidence that the dog is on point. When the puppy is first introduced to cover work he will most likely cast out of sight and remain away for a time. When he disappears for prolonged periods, remain in your tracks and do not resume hunting until he reappears. If he continues to remain away at frequent intervals, take him into strange country, allow him to cast out of sight, and then hide from him. Do not follow him, but cause him to hunt for you. Do not allow him to find you too quickly, and let him begin to feel that he is lost. A few experiences of this kind and he will learn that he must maintain a fairly close contact with you at all times.

The posting of an assistant, with whom the puppy is not acquainted, ahead of you in the cover to frighten the puppy back to you at intervals, can be utilized in some instances. This is not recommended generally, as it has the tendency to affect the puppy's boldness and independence. Always insist that he hunt for *you* and not for your companion. If he shows a preference for your companion, take him hunting by yourself frequently. And right here might be a good time to repeat the statement that the trainer must rely upon his own ingenuity on many occasions, for few dogs are temperamentally alike.

Occasionally we find young dogs that will not adopt a moderate range without drastic measures. It may be necessary to attach a long check cord to a youngster of this type, making him drag this through heavy cover. Give him as much as he will handle, and work him in this fashion for a time, gradually shortening the cord until he will handle properly without it. Some dogs will refuse to hunt when a check cord is attached. You may then apply other means, such as tying two sticks, one on each side of his collar and reaching to his forelegs. These will interfere with his progress, as they will rap him on the legs when he tries to bolt. A gunny sack attached to a short cord will also retard him without bruising him. These methods, however, have a tendency to reduce the dog's speed, and this is not desired.

The fact that the grouse dog's range should be more restricted than that of the quail and pheasant dog is no reason for there being any difference in the speed of the three types. The old-fashioned, plodding, methodical grouse dog has given way to the more energetic type, as scarcity of game and changes in the habits of these birds demand that the modern grouse dog cover much more territory in the course of a day's hunt. He should be fast, snappy in action, and possess a quality that seems to be born in some and acquired only after extensive experience by others. This is the ability to negotiate heavy cover and thick underbrush in a quiet, easy manner. He should also be decisive and positive on his points but should check his pace instantly upon catching the body scent of his quarry, roading to his game quietly and cautiously. The experienced grouse dog senses just how close he can get to the artful dodger of the woodlands.

The greatest percentage of shots at grouse is obtained

on birds that have flushed wild, or rather birds that are not directly flushed by the hunter. This bird seems to sense the approach of the gunner, no matter how quietly it be made, and will seldom lay for any considerable length of time to a dog's point. So it is necessary for the grouse hunter to begin to maneuver himself into position for a good shot the moment he sees his dog "making game." The approach to the point must be made in such a manner that the gun will have a fair chance should the grouse flush wild, for Old Biddy is using her brain and instinct every moment to plan her flight to safety.

All of this is by way of explaining the necessity for constant contact between master and dog. If the dog disappears over a slight rise and fails to show up presently, you should be able to feel that he is on point. But unless you are thoroughly familiar with this particular cover you are at a loss to know just how to approach this point. And even if you do know every foot of the territory you have no idea just where the dog is pointing. If, however, he is almost always in sight of you, you can watch him closely, see his first indications of the proximity of game, and lay your campaign accordingly. It has been said, and with a great deal of truth, that every grouse shot is different, and hence every approach to a point must take into consideration cover, vantage points, openings, wind, etc. Not every grouse hunter does this, but you can just bet that the old-timers do if they have time—and they do it pretty fast, too.

Older writers have contended that a grouse dog should be taught to turn *out* at the end of each cast. Most dogs turn out instinctively, but there are many that make a short loop toward their handler before straightening out on another quartering cast. To teach a dog to turn out at the end of each cast is a most difficult task and one that requires almost endless drilling. The dog must be brought to a complete stop every time he turns in, the handler must turn him completely around and send him on again. It may be necessary to repeat this procedure many times in a single workout, for it must be done until the dog instinctively makes an outward turn at the end of each cast. This is a more or less mechanical method and, in my opinion, is not worth the trouble. First, because it requires a great deal of handling, and too much whoaing and stopping and turning interfere with the dog's natural desire to hunt. Second, because the final accomplishment has a doubtful value.

It is admitted that it is a pretty sight to see a dog make the same outward turn every time he breaks his cast, but to the experienced eye it appears mechanical. It is also admitted that the dog that turns out is less liable to cast behind you. But this is its chief value. The dog that makes a short inward loop toward his master before swinging out on a new cast is apt to give his master more fair shots for this one reason: I have said that grouse often flush wild; they also most frequently flush *away* from the dog; thus, should a grouse be found on one of these short inward loops and flush wild before the dog can pin him, he is more apt to flush *away* from the dog, and consequently his natural line of flight might well be *toward* the gunner. For this reason I do not recommend that the amateur attempt to teach his dog to turn *out* at the end of each cast.

The writer is fully aware that this is a departure from the teachings of older writers, but this is not the first time, nor will it be the last, that disagreement with their instructions will be found in this book. I am definitely *not* an exponent of mechanical methods in field training and believe that the most valuable dog, no matter on what type of game bird he is to be used, will be the one that has been allowed to develop naturally.

So if he turns out or in, the main object is to have the

grouse dog hunt in front of you, quartering his course at good speed, and covering every likely spot. There can be no definite bounds to the grouse dog's range. It should be as wide or as restricted as the cover requires, for he should remain in sight of his master most of the time and hence maintain a fairly close contact. He should certainly handle kindly, responding to the low commands of his master, a soft whistle, or merely the wave of the hand.

Don't expect your puppy to develop into a top grouse dog the first season, nor the second. For this is the most difficult of all game birds to handle, and it is only through extensive experience that a dog becomes a master at this game.

Many grouse hunters attach a small bell to their dog's collar for cover work. This enables them to keep in constant contact with the dog, for the bell continues to tinkle until the dog stops. These accessories are especially valuable in dense cover or for use on a particularly wide dog. They do not seem to frighten the grouse.

The top grouse dog develops what seasoned grouse hunters call the "grouse weave," a manner of working his cover in a quartering way, weaving in and out, and taking in all likely spots, boring out ahead all the time—and doing this all in an exceedingly quiet manner. The good grouse dog seems fairly to tiptoe through the woods but always at a good pace.

The Woodcock Dog's Range

The woodcock dog is developed along the same lines as the grouse dog, but his requirements are not nearly so numerous. This is because of the great difference in the habits of the two birds, for woodcock will lay to a point much better than the grouse, pheasant, or even the quail.

Consequently the little fellow makes an excellent bird on which to train young dogs.

As the feeding habits of the woodcock limit his natural range to certain types of country, the main requirement of a good woodcock dog, other than a good nose, is control. He must work close to the gun, be willing to tackle heavy cover, and remain absolutely stanch on point. A dog that breaks at wing or shot is liable to flush a number of birds in his rush, as when the flight is on, one small cover can hold quite a number of boring woodcock. He must be particularly stanch because the cover in which he works is often so thick that considerable time is required for the gun to reach him. Many old-timers taught their woodcock dogs to flush on command after they had jockeyed themselves into a good shooting situation. If you are out strictly for meat, this may be condoned, but it is no small trick to train a dog in this manner, and I certainly do not recommend it, particularly for the amateur. I'll do my own flushing, please. On several occasions a companion and I, working with a beautifully mannered dog, have taken our limits of timber doodles from one small cover without sending the dog to retrieve until the last bird was down. Those were, frankly, memorable occasions, but many others have enjoyed similar experiences when the flight was on.

Chapter 10

THE FINISHING TOUCHES

❦

IN THE course of every dog's training there is a definite time when steps to finish him should be taken. This time is after he has begun to handle game properly. Until he has become thoroughly imbued with the desire to find game and is demonstrating a fair degree of stanchness on his points, no considerable amount of pressure should be employed to make him handle his game in a finished manner. The main objective should always be to have him develop in the natural way. Too much breaking at an early age will tend to cramp him and if the young dog is crowded too fast the danger of spoiling him is incurred.

Many a young dog has been ruined because he was forced to remain stanch and steady before he was thoroughly possessed with the desire to hunt. And, on the other hand, if too much levity is allowed over a lengthy period without correction, bad habits may be formed that may never be entirely corrected. So the time to take him in hand is after he begins to show a realization of his purpose in life.

Steadying to Shot and Wing

Let us say that the youngster is now hunting with much ambition and, while he is stanch on point, is still allowed to break shot and chase. This is the time to steady him to shot and wing.

I submitted this manuscript to a professional trainer who is a very close personal friend of mine. I have the utmost respect for his opinion and the highest confidence in his ability as a trainer. In fact, he has been training bird dogs for me for over twenty years and has solved some mighty knotty problems that were either beyond me or with which I had neither the time nor facilities to cope. I felt that he would take issue with me on my recommendation to allow young dogs to break to flush and chase on their first few points, for I know how careful he is on this matter. I, too, believe in keeping the young dog steady *if you can*, but if this is not possible I do not want him punished for breaking the first few times. My trainer-friend has an assistant, of course, who can flush the birds while he handles the young dog. This is not always possible with the amateur, and for that reason the amateur cannot always flush the birds and keep the young dog steady at the same time.

My friend's criticism warrants quoting here, for what he has to say is backed by a lifetime of experience. His ability as a trainer is so well known and his services so sought after that he never has to advertise and always has a waiting list. In regard to steadying to shot and wing he wrote:

Right here is where I believe that I must take issue with you. I understand that you are advising the amateur trainer to shoot over his young dog's points up to this time, allowing the dog to break shot and chase. If the dog has shown some tenderness on his game or to the gun to warrant this procedure, all right, but with the average dog that has developed normally up to the stage of the game where he is pointing with a fair degree of stanchness I would never think of shooting over one of his points unless I were in position to steady him. A dog that has never been allowed to break shot is almost sure to be easy to keep steady, but one that has tasted the sweets of shot breaking is pretty sure to be a problem always. More especially for an amateur who is trying to handle his dog and shoot birds at the same time. I realize that you are trying to steer clear of the overtrained, mechanical dog and trying to teach your amateur readers to allow a dog to develop naturally and I think that your point is mighty well taken. I agree with you most heartily in most instances, but you and I know that steadiness to shot and wing is NOT, has never been, and never will be a natural instinct with any dog living. That part of his education *must be mechanical* and for that mechanism to work smoothly I contend that it is best for the normal young dog to break shot just as few times as possible. If it should become apparent to the handler that his pupil is becoming stale or overtrained he can allow or even encourage him to break and chase for a time, but let him leave off shooting until he is ready to begin keeping the dog steady again.

I have seen too many young dogs that I have trained myself and turned over to their amateur handlers stanch and steady to shot. These owners, after shooting over the dog for the two months or so of open season, return the dog to me to resteady to shot. Ninety-nine out of every hundred are never reliably steady again after the two months of shot breaking. Never anywhere near so steady as before they were ever allowed to break shot.

I believe that the rather drastic measures that you are advocating to cure the young dog of shot breaking (while they are O.K. if you have a real shot breaker to deal with) will be just as likely to cramp and take the edge off a young dog's enthusiasm as my plan of simply never allowing him to break shot in the beginning, and the latter plan is so much easier and simpler for the handler.

These are wise words, to be sure, and if the beginner can keep his young dog from breaking and chasing in the beginning, that is indeed the thing to do. It is best to take a companion along to flush the birds for you while you handle the young pupil, until he comes to realize that he must remain stanch at the flush of the birds. But don't use too much force.

If, however, he gets away from you a number of times and comes to like this business of breaking and chasing too much, these rather drastic methods my friend refers to must be employed if you want him steady to shot. Some hunters prefer that their dogs break shot to retrieve, as the chances of losing a cripple are lessened.

Get the dog on point. Go to him and handle him as usual, stroking him along the back. Attach a check cord thirty to forty feet long to his collar and grasp the other end firmly. Flush the birds and shoot. He will dash forward to chase. When he reaches the full length of the cord he will probably be running at full speed. Then is the time to throw your full weight against the cord, backward. The dog will probably change ends in the air and fall upon his back. Lay down your gun and draw him in to you, hand over hand. Force him down by tapping him with the whip. Retain your grip on the cord and, walking all around him, repeat the command "Whoa." Tap him with the whip every time he attempts to rise. Hold him in this position for a short time. Then deliberately reload, unsnap the cord from his collar, and resume hunting. Repeat this lesson in the first workout if possible. This may sound pretty drastic, but you should use your own judgment as to how drastic it should be.

This should be attempted first when the dog is pointing in an open space, as he will then be allowed to run the full length of the cord at full speed, and will get the full benefit of the shock. If he is a bold youngster, this is what you want. If the point is established near a small tree, walk around the tree with the cord, coming back in front to flush the birds. In this manner the dog can be upset before he reaches you and will not associate you with the jerk.

He will probably run the full length of the cord two or

three times, and then may chase only a short way. He is now coming into hand. In his next workout omit the cord. He will most likely realize that the cord is not attached and break shot when the birds are flushed. Drop a handkerchief or your hat to mark the spot, and go get him. Do not call him back, but take him by the collar and lead him back to the spot in which he pointed. Force him down by tapping him with the whip and walk around him, repeating the command "Whoa." If he persists in rising, tap him a bit harder, snap your cord to his collar, and tie it to a bush. Keep him down for a time, reload your gun, pat him a few times, and resume hunting.

The object now is to get him on point as often as possible, always bringing him back and administering light punishment when he breaks shot. The more points you secure, the sooner he will be a broken dog. If he continues to break badly, upset him at the end of the long cord two or three times and start all over again. Do not caution him when the shot is fired, as he might interpret this to mean that he is privileged to break shot when the command is omitted. Simply hold out the whip when the shot is fired.

It is extremely difficult to keep a dog steady to shot and shoot birds over him at the same time, for most of us are prone to break shot ourselves when a bird falls. The only way to keep your dog steady is to remain steady yourself.

Do not dash in whenever a bird falls, but remain in your tracks and watch your dog for signs of uneasiness. By dashing in to pick up a fallen bird, you are only encouraging your dog to do likewise and you will soon find that he will beat you to it. Then your work will have been undone. In hunting with a companion, caution him to remain still after shooting until you have sent your dog on.

The field manners of a hunter are generally reflected in the manners of his shooting dog. If you desire your dog to remain steady to wing and shot, it is absolutely necessary that you remain steady to wing and shot yourself. Particular care must be taken with the dog that naturally loves to retrieve. The sight of a falling bird proves a stronger temptation to him than to one that has not been allowed to retrieve.

It is the common tendency of the quail and pheasant hunter, particularly the ringneck fan because of the habits of the bird, to step forward immediately after the shot is fired, and consequently few of them are ever able to keep a dog steady to shot and wing. In fact, many hunters make no effort to prevent their dogs from breaking shot to retrieve and, indeed, this fault sometimes has its virtues. Many crippled birds, particularly pheasants, which are strong runners and carry a lot of lead, are recovered quickly by shot-breaking dogs; but, on the other hand, these same dogs inadvertently flush many "sleepers" before the gunner has an opportunity to reload.

Steady to shot and wing is a nicety of training that shows finish and is to be preferred. Some sportsmen require their dogs to find and point dead birds but do not allow them to retrieve. These dogs are more apt to remain steady to shot and wing, but retrieving is to be preferred, especially in country where thick briars are abundant.

In teaching steady to shot and wing, work your dog alone. There is a bit of jealousy in the make-up of some dogs that causes them to commit deliberate errors when worked in company. Some dogs will display excellent manners when worked alone, but become so upset by the spirit of competition that they will flush and chase birds when another dog is near. So take no chances and work your dog alone.

Dropping to Flush and Shot

If he persists in being unsteady to flush after numerous lessons, it will be well to teach him to drop to flush and shot. Some trainers recommend the teaching of this in all cases, as it induces steadiness and keeps the dog under better control. This is true, but the dog that stands to flush not only looks better but is able to mark down birds with better accuracy. Also, the dog that drops to shot and wing is sometimes inclined to drop on point, which detracts from his performance.

I do not recommend that this be taught to timid dogs, however, as the application of more force is required.

The dog should stop or drop to accidental flush, however. To teach him this you must be constantly on the alert and take advantage of every error the dog makes. When he accidentally or otherwise flushes game, give the command "Drop." He will probably chase, so mark the spot, catch him, lead him back to the place, and force him down with light taps of the whip, repeating the command "Drop." Walk around him as before, making him remain down for a time. If the flush has been deliberate, you might sting him a bit with the whip. Take advantage of every opportunity that presents itself, and soon he will drop instantly every time he makes such an error.

Dropping to shot can be more easily taught in the yard, by using a small-caliber pistol. Make him drop every time you give the command "Drop." Then accompany the command with gunfire. He will soon associate the two and drop at the firing of the gun as well as at the command. You will then no longer need to use the command in the field when you are shooting over him.

Backing

Backing, or honoring another dog's point, is really an expression of the pointing instinct. The average dog will back instinctively, especially if he has been raised with his brothers and sisters and has watched them point butterflies and grasshoppers. Others are inclined to be jealous and must be made to back to prevent them from stealing their brace mate's point.

I know one field-trial handler who never taught any of his dogs to back. When asked for a reason he said: "You can't win a field trial backing." This is true, but field-trial requirements, in the matter of finish, are growing more rigid as time goes on, and the dog that is detected in a refusal to back is charged with a serious error.

In teaching your dog to back, always select a thoroughly finished brace mate and one in which your dog will have full confidence. Never take him out with a false-pointing dog, or he will soon lose confidence and begin moving up to investigate for himself.

Get the brace mate on point. Call the young dog and, if possible, work him up into such a position that he will not catch scent of the birds, but will come upon the pointing dog suddenly. As soon as he catches sight of the pointing dog, call his name sharply. The surprise of seeing the other dog on point and hearing his name called at the same instant will probably cause him to check his stride and stiffen up into a point. Go to him, stroke him along the back, as usual, and have an assistant flush the birds while you remain at the side of your own dog. Once he has backed a pointing dog and has seen the birds flushed to the other's point, he will soon acquire the habit of backing without much effort on your part.

If he refuses to back and goes in ahead until he has got

the bird scent himself, do not try to correct him there, but flush the birds and await another occasion. The next time the brace mate points, attach a check cord to your dog and work him toward the birds from such a direction as to make scenting conditions most unfavorable for him. As soon as he catches sight of the pointing dog, check him and tie him to a bush or sapling. Let him watch the other dog. Do not lead him in so close that he will smell the birds himself, for he must learn to back from any distance. He must stop as soon as he catches sight of the pointing dog, no matter whether he can smell the birds or not.

After a few lessons, try having him tense up on point, but caution him in a low tone, checking him and stroking him gently while he is watching the pointing dog. A little patient repetition of this lesson will produce the desired results. Speak his name sharply each time he catches sight of the pointing dog, and he will soon learn to back at command. This is of value when the pointing dog cannot be seen easily on account of high cover and your dog is in danger of flushing the birds by coming down wind.

Blinking

Blinking is a man-made fault and one of the most difficult to correct. A blinker is a dog that will find game, point it, and leave it before his handler arrives; or one that will find game, refuse to point it, veer off from it to avoid flushing, and then resume hunting.

The fault often accompanies gun-shyness, and is generally brought on by too severe handling in an endeavor to break the young dog. Hence, every care should be taken to prevent the pupil from associating game birds with punishment. and the trainer should not be in too big a hurry to apply the finishing touches.

There are several degrees of blinking that can be corrected by careful handling. There is the dog that refuses to stand still on his points. He will circle the birds, pointing them from the other side, and will not allow his handler to shoot directly over him. This is not blinking in the true sense of the term and can be prevented by always approaching the dog from the front so that he will be facing you. Another way is to teach him to drop at command or signal. As soon as he points, or before he has had an opportunity to shift his position, have him drop and keep him there until you have flushed the birds. Constant and careful work in this manner will bring him about.

There is also the dog that will point his birds stanchly but, upon the approach of his handler, will back away and slink back to the trainer, remaining at heel while the birds are flushed. This dog has had an unfortunate experience in his early training and associates the flush of birds with some form of punishment. Or the sound of flushing birds may be distasteful to him. The best way to correct the faults in this dog is to hunt him with a bold dog that breaks shot and chases badly. Encourage him to break and chase likewise, and teach him to retrieve. If you can induce him to break and chase, he will soon lose his fear of birds and will lose his uneasiness on point.

The dog that carefully sidesteps his birds and resumes hunting without showing any desire to point them presents a discouraging problem. It is best to dispose of him as worthless rather than to attempt to overcome this fault, for the chances of success are poor, at best. This is blinking in its worst form.

Bolting

A confirmed bolter is a dog that refuses to handle, pays no attention to his handler, and simply goes out of the country on self-hunting expeditions until his thirst for hunting is assuaged. He then returns home by himself. A dog of this type is generally too much for an amateur, and it is best to turn him over to a professional who has the assistants and facilities to work him.

A good way to cure him, however, is to take him hunting every day, keeping him on the lead all the time, bringing him in to back other dogs, and allowing him to watch the shooting. Allow him to find the dead birds, keeping him always on the lead. Give him an occasional bird's head to eat. Fondle the other hunting dogs in front of him, but never allow him to hunt. He will most likely begin to realize that he will derive more pleasure out of hunting for you than by himself, and will start serving the gun.

A quicker way, probably, is to provide yourself with two well-mounted assistants, each riding on different sides of the area. Cast the dog away and when he disappears continue to blow one long blast of the whistle. Should he go to the right, the assistant on that side will ride him down and whip him back toward you. Should he cross the course to the left, the other assistant will repeat the process. A number of lessons of this sort will bring him to his senses, and he will begin to pay attention to the whistle. This method is not recommended to the amateur, as many dogs are spoiled in this manner, and the correcting of this fault requires the hand of the experienced professional trainer.

Trailing

A trailer is a dog that continually follows his brace mate. Such a dog should be worked alone at all times. As many birds as possible should be killed over him to increase his interest in independent hunting, and he should never be put down with another dog until he evidences intense interest in hunting. Sometimes punishment will break him of this habit, but it is best to work him alone.

Cutting Back

The dog that cuts back is one that makes a cast and then turns and comes straight back toward his handler. This is a worthless habit and should be discouraged in the puppy as soon as any evidence of it is seen. When the puppy starts to cut back, trot toward him with upraised hand, blowing two short blasts on the whistle frequently, and encouraging him to go out as soon as possible. Never pet him when he comes back to you in this fashion. Pay no attention to him except to encourage him to resume hunting. Quicken your pace the minute you see him start to cut back. This will shorten the distance between you, and he will soon realize that you intend to maintain contact with him without his cutting back to find you.

A bag of small pebbles is sometimes carried by trainers who work dogs of this type. Whenever the dog comes in close, a pebble is tossed at him and he learns that he will be peppered with those small stones if he cuts in too much. He begins to associate the throwing of the pebble with the raising of the hand, and accepts that as a signal to turn out and resume hunting. This method is not recommended for timid dogs, however, and the amateur must use judgment in its employment.

Chapter 11

GUN-SHYNESS

❧

GUN-SHYNESS is not an inherited fault, although disposition or temperament may contribute to its acquisition. Extreme caution must be exercised in introducing the gun to the timid dog, and no liberties should be taken with any puppy simply because he shows a bold nature.

The best cure for gun-shyness lies in prevention. If the gun is gradually brought into play at feeding time (see Chapter 3) and care taken in introducing it in the field, there is little likelihood that this fault will develop. But the boldest of puppies can be made gun-shy if the trainer indulges in reckless habits at the wrong time.

There are several degrees of gun-shyness: One dog will tuck his tail and bolt for home when the first shot is fired; another will come to heel when the shot is fired but resume hunting after a time. Careful handling will generally bring such dogs around in a little while.

The toughest customer of all is the dog that merely sulks and quits hunting when the gun is fired. He isn't particularly afraid, certainly isn't panicky, for he will generally come to heel and walk along with you. He just doesn't like gunfire and he won't hunt. And there is no way to *make* a dog *actually* hunt. This dog should be discarded by the amateur, unless he shows immediate progress, and unusual promise, for the trainer can best employ his time in the development of better material.

In breaking the gun-shy dog, the trainer must convey to him that the gun means him no harm, is a definite part of hunting, and is closely associated with his pleasure afield. The dog is afraid of the gun because the noise it makes is something to which he is not accustomed, and he must be brought to realize that it is directly related to hunting. Even then he may not like it, but once he comes to associate the shot with fallen birds, from which an occasional head may be given him, the worst is over.

The dog that comes to heel but resumes hunting after a while is the easiest to cure. For this fellow it is best not to associate gunfire with the flight of game birds for a while. Just shoot when he is off on a good cast and is interested in hunting. Pay no attention to him when he comes to heel. Never shoot when he is close by. Firing the gun two or three times during a workout is sufficient. He will soon learn that the gun means him no harm. Don't shoot over his points until he has had considerable experience on game and loves to hunt. Never take him up when he is at heel. Always wait until he resumes hunting.

A good method of curing gun-shyness calls for the use of other dogs. Simply lead the dog around behind a couple of hunters, or, if you are hunting by yourself, a small boy can take care of the gun-shy dog. Lead him up in sight of the pointing dog, but stop at a good distance away. Let him watch the shooting. After a few points he can be brought up closer. At first he will be quite unhappy about it, but after a time he will begin to show signs of interest in what the other dogs are doing, particularly if you make much over them and pay no attention to him.

It will be well to lead him up behind a shot-breaking dog. This shows him plainly that the other dog has no fear of the gun. When he begins to show some interest in the work, allow him to find the dead birds and retrieve them. Give him an occasional bird's head to eat. Do not allow him to hunt, however, but keep him on the lead until he has lost his fear of the gun. Some dogs are of such jealous natures that this method will effect a cure quickly. The dog that is slightly gun-shy may be worked with absorbent cotton in his ears. This is sometimes somewhat difficult to keep in place, however. Decrease the amount as he shows improvement, until none is used.

Taking the dog to trap and skeet shoots is recommended in some instances. If you adopt this method, tie the dog to a stake or bench and sit down beside him. Adopt an indifferent attitude toward the shooting, chat with your friends, and pay no attention to the dog when he makes efforts to escape. Attempts to reassure him will only aggravate his fear, and your calm unconcern will impart confidence to him. When he observes that you are indifferent to the noise, he will come to realize that there is nothing for him to fear.

I do not recommend this method except in emergencies, for generally there is a crowd in attendance at these shoots, and there will be several well-intentioned persons who will likely come over and want to pet the dog out of sympathy, thereby frustrating your efforts. So stay away from the crowd. Take a friend along who will show the dog no attention. Sit down and chat as if no guns were being fired.

The "starvation" method is probably the most effective of all. In the experience of many professionals it has worked in extreme cases more often than it has failed. It will usually work for anyone who will not get discouraged and discontinue it too soon.

Place the dog in the kennel and allow him to go without food for twenty-four hours. Place his pan in the kennel yard, walk off a short distance, and when he begins to eat fire a shot from a small pistol or lightly loaded gun. He will probably leave his food and dash back into his kennel. Remove the food and leave him. Try him again in five or six hours. In some cases the dog will dash at the pan, bolt a couple of mouthfuls, and go for his kennel as soon as the shot is fired. To prevent this, fire the shot before he reaches the pan. As soon as he leaves the food, remove it. Always keep plenty of fresh water in the kennel, but do not allow him to eat except when the gun is being fired. If he will remain long enough to snatch a couple of mouthfuls you are making progress, and it is only a case of time before he will allow you to shoot several times while he is eating. Keep him hungry, and gradually decrease the distance between him and the gun. Soon you can fire directly over him. Even after the dog shows no fear of the gun while eating, you should continue to be careful with him in the field. Take no chances, for frequently dogs will eat under the gun and continue to show fear of it in the field. Never fire but one shot over a slightly gun-shy dog in the field. Take him along by easy stages. Give him all the bird work you can, for the quickest way to cure a gun-shy dog is to develop the hunting instinct to the highest degree and kill birds for him.

In this connection the experience of Edward Farrior, the well-known Alabama trainer, with the setter Champion Jay R's Boy, is worthy of mention here. Boy came to Farrior as a man-shy, bird-shy, and gun-shy dog immediately after his derby year, during which he had won the American Field Futurity. The dog possessed a world of style and stamina in the field but was practically a worthless dog in his present mental condition. Farrior made a companion of him that summer, taking him along everywhere he went. He made friends with him, and the dog regained his confidence in mankind.

When the training season started, Boy was not allowed to hunt. He was given into the charge of a Negro boy, who kept him on a lead and followed behind Farrior as he schooled other candidates for field-trial honors. Day after day this procedure was followed.

Finally, Farrior killed a bird at short range, the load of shot damaging it. He tossed this to Boy, who gulped it down. After a while, Farrior fed him another, and the dog began to take an interest in the gun. Thereafter he was given every bird's head to eat, and within a short time he was again placed in training, showing no fear of game or gun. His subsequent field-trial record, a brilliant one in which he won the National Free-for-All Championship twice, proved the worth of these lessons.

J. Earl Bufkin, the noted Mississippi trainer, once broke a gun-shy setter named Shiek by adopting a novel method. The usually successful starvation method failed to effect a cure, and the dog was apparently hopeless. As a court of last resort, Bufkin took the dog down near a pond that was frequented every afternoon by numbers of doves. The open season was on. Bufkin staked the dog in the open, and as the birds came into water he shot several, one of them falling close to the trembling setter. The dog momentarily forgot his fear and made a lunge for the bird. Bufkin, who had about given up the job as a hopeless task, was encouraged. Every afternoon he took the dog to the same place and held his fire until he could drop the birds close to the dog. Within a short time the dog was entirely over his gun-shyness and was retrieving to the gun as well as one would desire.

Chapter 12

RETRIEVING

❦

THERE ARE two methods of teaching a dog to retrieve. One is the system of natural retrieving, which is developed in a spirit of playfulness. In this, no force is employed, for the method simply consists of encouraging the puppy to chase a rubber ball and return with it until such procedure becomes a pleasant pastime to him. Gloves, other objects, and finally dead birds can be substituted for the ball, and the desire to retrieve will be so developed that the dog will hunt for objects that have been thrown into the cover or otherwise hidden from him.

Some dogs take to this readily and make excellent retrievers in the field. The objection to the method, however, lies in the fact that the dog will retrieve only when he is so disposed. The time you need this accomplishment the most may be the time he will refuse. You then have no method of *making* him conform to your will.

The other method is known as the force system. In it the application of a certain amount of force is absolutely necessary, for the dog must be made to realize that punishment will follow his refusal to retrieve. The most reliable retrievers are those developed through the force system, and the various faults accompanying this accomplishment can be corrected through this method.

Many amateur and some professional trainers maintain that a bird dog should not be taught or even allowed to retrieve. They contend that this proficiency induces unsteadiness to shot and pottering about in search of imaginary game. This is undoubtedly true in some instances, but the natural retriever is much more likely to break shot to retrieve than the dog that has gained this talent through force training. The trainer who constantly controls *himself* can keep a retrieving dog steady as easily as he can one that does not have this talent. Retrieving is a nice accomplishment, valuable in any type of country, and an outright necessity in some sections.

Natural Retrieving

It is best to start lessons in natural retrieving when the puppy is at a tender age. Then the spirit of play is uppermost in the puppy, and while these exercises are really lessons, he should, for a time, look upon them as playtimes.

Take the puppy out of his kennel yard and onto a smooth lawn or into a quiet room, where no other dogs are present and where he will not be distracted. Bounce a soft rubber ball in front of him several times, gaining his interest and attention. Then roll it along the lawn or floor for a few feet in front of him. Give the command "Fetch." He will most likely chase the ball, catch it, and return to you with it. Take it from him, pet him, reward him with a tidbit, such as a small piece of cooked liver, and throw the ball again. Repeat this a number of times, always repeating the command "Fetch." The puppy will not understand this command at first, but will gradually come to associate it with the tossing of the ball. This will be all for the first lesson for you must stop before he becomes tired or disinterested. These lessons must be conducted in a spirit of playfulness and should be ended before there is any laxity of interest.

Repeat them every day and presently the puppy will begin to look forward to them. After he has shown a growing interest in retrieving the ball, substitute an old glove. This will be soft to his mouth, and he will enjoy shaking it. Always reward him with a caress or tiny morsel. If he shows no enthusiasm for the glove, rub a bit of meat on the outside and place a piece inside, closing the wrist with a bit of string to prevent the young pupil from securing it.

Allow him to smell the glove, toss it out, and you will find that his interest has been renewed. When he picks up the glove, call him to you, repeating the command "Fetch." Always reward him when he brings it to you.

The puppy will almost invariably dash after any object thrown and will pick it up, but he will often drop it before he returns it to you. If he fails to bring it to you, do not reward him. Go with him to the object, place it in his mouth, and persuade him to carry it back to the starting place. Then take it from him and reward him generously. It is well that you frequently change objects for him to retrieve, for he may become so accustomed to the glove and the ball that he will retrieve no other. After he has shown considerable progress, you may use a dead bird, keeping its wings strapped close to the body with rubber bands or string.

Short lessons given several times a day over a considerable period, and the puppy will progress to the point where he can be induced to hunt for hidden objects. Up to this time he has depended upon his eyes instead of his sense of smell.

After he has become proficient in retrieving from short distances, increase these distances gradually, finally tossing the object into high cover. This will cause him to rely on his nose. If he races past the object, allow him to hunt for a while and then, before he loses interest, call him in to you and help him find it, repeating the words "Seek dead." He will soon learn to take your wave of the hand as a direction and will hunt until he finds the object without assistance. He can then be gradually worked into hunting for hidden objects that he has not seen thrown.

In these advanced lessons, it is best to allow him to retrieve from short distances for a few times before giving him more difficult tasks. In having him retrieve game it will be well to place a check cord on him for the first few times. This will allow you to pull him in to you as soon as he has picked up the bird. Never allow him to play with the bird, for he will then develop the habit of mouthing or chewing it.

Remember that every lesson should be short, no matter how great the enthusiasm of the pupil. As there is no force attached to this training, it is imperative that the puppy's enthusiasm for these sessions should be maintained. Never allow him to grow tired, and always stop when he has done an especially nice piece of retrieving.

If the puppy is reluctant to release the object, a slight pressure on the upper lip will force the flesh against the teeth, causing pain. This will make him open his mouth. The object should be removed without delay, the pressure released, and the puppy petted. In administering this slight punishment, always precede it with the command "Give." The puppy will in time associate this command with releasing the object, and no further punishment will be necessary.

Force Retrieving

Force retrieving means just what the name implies. The dog must be *forced* to respond to the commands of the trainer and retrieve promptly even though he may not be in the mood for this type of work. There are several methods of teaching force retrieving. All will produce the desired results if the trainer will follow the various steps in each patiently and persistently, and exercise good judgment in administering punishment. Each method calls for a certain amount of force, applied, however, in different manners. The general principles of each are the same and the methods of procedure, except in minor instances, are practically identical.

In every system, the dog is taken through successive steps: First, he is caused to hold the object in his mouth; then to carry it around while walking at the side of the trainer; in the next step he will learn to *take* the object from the hand, then pick it up from the ground; finally he is taught to "fetch" the object from varying distances, and to give it into the hand of the trainer.

In this form of training the beginner will do well to proceed with the greatest care. It is best to start after the dog has had some experience in the field. Because methods of force are involved, the trainer continually runs the risk of breaking the dog's spirit and retarding his development in field work. Some dogs respond quickly, while others become obstinate and sullen. With an individual of the latter type, the beginner must be especially careful, for there will be many times that his patience is taxed to the utmost. He cannot afford to give vent to his feelings and inflict severe punishment on the dog, for this generally erases the progress he has made and may have the effect of causing the dog to become permanently cowed. Adopt a humane method and proceed slowly. More time and less punishment will produce the best results.

Perhaps the most generally known method of teaching force retrieving calls for the use of the spike collar. There are several types of these collars on the market, some less severe than others. In the hands of an experienced trainer, who knows when to stop and how far to go with punishment, these collars are quite efficient. But when used by a quick-tempered, inexperienced man they can become instruments of torture, producing more harm than good. I cannot recommend them for general use by the novice.

Two other methods in common use are those in which the force is applied by pinching the dog's ear between the thumb and finger and by squeezing the forepaw with one hand. These are humane and effective methods and will produce excellent results when carefully employed. In these more time is generally required than in the spike-collar system, but the novice is less liable to inflict too much pain.

The Webster Price Method

The most efficient method I have ever seen is that employed by a well-known Southern professional trainer. In 1916, an energetic young man, broken in health, was advised by his doctor that he could not recover unless he spent most of his time outdoors. His lifetime hobby had been upland game hunting. He had developed and trained a number of good shooting dogs of his own and had quite a local reputation as an amateur trainer.

In 1920, Webster Price moved his family to Iuka, Mississippi, and opened his own bird-dog training school. Success attended him from the first. His quiet, sincere manner won many friends for him, his training ability was reflected in the performance of his dogs, and within a few years he was a familiar figure around the major field-trial circuit. Price developed sixteen winners within three years, among them being the triple champion pointer, Dan Woolton's Dauntless. A home-loving person, devoted to his family, he found the protracted absences necessitated by field-trial competition irksome, and settled down to training shooting dogs exclusively on his Mississippi preserve. His system of teaching force retrieving is here given to the public *for the first time.*

The Webster Price Retrieving Yoke

In this system, Mr. Price uses what he is pleased to term "the retrieving yoke." The yoke is simple in construction and anyone can make it. It consists of a three-quarter-inch board, two feet and nine inches long and two and three-fourths inches wide. The board should be planed down smooth on all sides.

Whittle out a handle to fit the hand. Bore a small hole in the board about one inch from the wide end and another six inches below the first. Knot one end of a length of small window cord some thirty inches long, pass the cord through both holes so that a loop is formed under the board. Adjust the length of the cord to suit by looping or knotting, and the yoke is ready for use.

The yoke has a varied purpose. It is slipped over the dog's head, the cord underneath his throat and the board on top of his neck. When the cord is jerked, the pressure causes the dog to open his mouth, allowing the trainer to place the "buck" therein. The yoke is humane, can be used as a lead, the dog's head can be raised or lowered as desired, and it is effective with the most obstinate pupil without inflicting severe punishment. The dog is under complete control all the time the yoke is on his neck. A tightening of the cord generally produces enough pressure to obtain proper results, but a slight twist on the handle will force the edge of the board against the back of the dog's neck, and additional pressure is obtained.

In addition to the yoke, equip yourself with one or several retrieving bucks. These objects can take almost any form. A good buck to use at first is a clean corncob. It will soil easily but can be replaced daily. A corncob around which feathers have been tied flatwise makes an excellent buck in simulation of a bird.

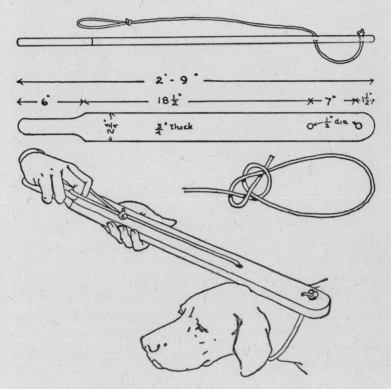

The Webster Price Retrieving Yoke

A set of bucks that will serve the purpose best, however, is made in the following manner: From an old broom handle saw three lengths, each about eight inches long; sew a clean piece of canvas around one of these lengths, drawing the cloth tight, and having the cover fit snugly. This is the plain buck and one for use in the first lessons.

Bore two small holes, close together and at right angles, near each end of another length. Drive tenpenny nails through these holes so that the buck will be in the center of the nails. The buck will then take the shape of a sawhorse. Wooden pegs may be substituted for the nails to lighten the buck. Sew a canvas covering over the broom handle, slitting the ends of the cloth and drawing them around the nails or pegs, sewing the ends tightly. This buck is now so fastened as to aid the dog in picking it up from the ground or floor and is to be used after the dog has become proficient in his first lessons.

Cut several pieces of wire almost as long as the third length of broom handle and staple this lengthwise to the wood at even intervals. Cover this with canvas. This is the "hard-mouthed" buck and is to be used only when the dog shows a tendency to bite down too hard on the plain buck or sawhorse. You may never find any use for it, as few dogs will try to chew such a hard substance as a broom handle, but it is well to have it handy in the event that he should show hard-mouthed tendencies. If he begins to close down on the plain bucks, simply substitute the one that is reinforced with wire. The surprise he will receive will soon teach him that all objects must be handled tenderly.

Each buck should be washed and thoroughly cleaned every time it is used.

The First Step

If the weather is hot, every lesson should be given during the cool part of the day, when the dog is breathing naturally and with his mouth closed. Do not attempt force retrieving during the open season. At that time concentrate on field training.

The first step consists of merely getting the dog accustomed to wearing the yoke and holding the buck in his mouth. Take him into a cool, quiet room or yard where you will not be disturbed. Put the yoke on the dog's neck, talking to him in a kindly tone. Sit down beside him and slip the yoke on and off his neck. After he becomes accustomed to it, have him walk beside you for a while, using the yoke as a lead. Finally seat yourself beside him, the plain buck in the left hand, the handle of the yoke in the right.

Hold out the buck before him and give the command "Fetch." Tighten the cord with short jerks, and the instant he opens his mouth release the pressure and place the buck between his jaws. Quickly place one hand under his jaw and the other on top of his head, stroking him a while, talking to him in kindly tones. The purpose of this lesson is to get him to hold the buck in his mouth.

The handle of the yoke should be held with the thumb and third and little fingers, the cord being jerked with the index and middle fingers. Short jerks are more effective than long pulls. Anyone can use the yoke properly with a little practice.

When the dog drops the buck, pick it up, apply the pressure in short jerks, give the command "Fetch," and replace the buck, releasing the pressure immediately and stroking him as before. Repeat this a number of times, but do not allow the lessons to last more than fifteen minutes.

Some dogs take to this work readily and will hold the buck for a considerable length of time during the first lessons. Others resent the pressure and require more time.

After a few lessons you will be able to have the dog walk along by your side, holding the buck in his mouth. The dog will enjoy walking about, as it serves to work off nervous tension. Do not proceed to the next step until you have made this progress. If you proceed carefully and conduct yourself in a firm but kindly manner, the dog will have no fear of the yoke and in a short time will not be averse to holding the buck and being led about while holding the object. This lesson lays the ground work for what is to follow and should be repeated every day for a week or more. In taking the buck from the dog always repeat the command "Give." If the dog is reluctant to release the buck, place added emphasis on the command and tighten the cord. He will soon come to associate the word "Give" with the pressure and will respond to the command.

Reaching for It

The next step is to teach the dog to reach for the buck when the handler holds it in front of him. This is done by jerking the cord, repeating the command "Fetch," and giving the dog's head a little push toward the buck. As soon as he reaches for the buck, release the pressure and lead him about with the buck in his mouth. Repeat this daily for a number of times and do not proceed with other lessons until he will reach for it when the word "Fetch" is spoken and no pressure applied.

After he has shown progress in these lessons, change the position of the buck by holding it to one side of him or higher and lower than his head. Always allow him to see it, however. Release the pressure the instant he reaches for the buck, and always reward him with pats and kind words when he performs well.

Picking It Up

Now advance the dog to lessons in picking up the object from the ground or floor. In these lessons, the sawbuck is used as this will allow the dog to take hold of it with more ease. The trainer holds the yoke in *both hands* this time, as this will allow him more control over the dog. Place the sawhorse buck on the floor a foot or so in front of the dog. Give the command "Fetch" at the same time, and push the dog forward with the yoke. If he picks up the buck, all well and good, but if he refuses, lower his head by pressing downward on the yoke until the dog's nose is on the buck. Repeat the word "Fetch," move the buck slightly with the toe of the shoe, and jerk the cord until he grabs the buck. If he refuses, speak a bit roughly, giving the command "Fetch," thrust the buck in the dog's mouth, and lead him about, making him carry it. Stroke the dog and encourage him with kind words, but he must be made to carry the buck while he is being led about. Give him a short rest and repeat the lesson.

It may require much repetition before he will pick up the buck at the command, but continue to work with him in a firm but kind manner. After he will pick up the buck readily have him hold it in his mouth while being led around by the yoke. During all the retrieving lessons this walking around will serve to rest him and will help convince him that you have him under control.

Never work the dog more than fifteen minutes at a time. This lesson must be repeated until the dog will pick up the buck willingly and carry it about for a considerable distance while being led by the yoke.

Then toss the buck out a short distance from him. Lead

him to it by the yoke, repeating the command "Fetch." When he picks it up, lead him back to the starting point, take the buck from him, and pet him lavishly.

Gradually increase the distance, always allowing the dog to see you toss the buck. After a while he will begin to show signs of wanting to go for the buck of his own volition. Be sure, however, that he is proficient in this department before he is allowed to go by himself. Substitute the plain buck for the sawhorse and work him with that for a while. Always reward him when he does a good job.

Fetching

Now that he shows a willingness to go after the buck, the next step is to work him without the yoke. For this, the handler attaches only a cord some ten or twelve feet long to his collar. Often the dog attempts to take advantage of the change by disobedience. If he disregards the command "Fetch," jerk on the cord several times. If he continues to disobey, place the yoke on him again and force him to fetch. He will soon realize that his disobedience will mean that he must wear the yoke again. The fetching and carrying about now goes on daily, with only a cord on the dog. Always remember that the lessons must be short and that the dog must be rewarded for good work.

Now you approach the final stage of the training. The dog must be worked without the cord. It is best to give these lessons in an enclosure so the dog cannot escape. Have him take the plain buck from your hand and hold it for a while. Take it from him and toss it out in plain sight of him. Give the command "Fetch." When he returns with it, allow him to hold it for a time, stroking him and talking kindly to him all the while. Always pet him lavishly and show your pleasure when he performs correctly. When he refuses to do your bidding the yoke must again be brought into use. Repeat these lessons daily until he will retrieve promptly from considerable distances.

It is advisable to substitute a dead bird for the buck occasionally, and especially at this stage of training. A pigeon will serve the purpose, and the bird's wings should be tied closely to its body. If the dog shows a tendency toward being hard-mouthed on birds, space a few nails about the bird's body, securely tying them in place by wrapping the body with string. In introducing the bird to him it will be well to work him for the first few times with a light line attached to his collar, as this will allow you to prevent him from mouthing the bird.

Seeking Dead

After the dog has learned to fetch on command, he should be taught to "Seek Dead." Hide the plain buck in the grass. Take the dog to this vicinity, attach the light check cord to his collar, and start hunting for the buck while repeating the words "Seek Dead." It will be necessary for you to show much interest in this work yourself, in order to convey the spirit of it to the dog. Bend over and search the ground and bushes, repeating the words "Seek Dead." Allow the dog to find the buck. When you are sure he sees it, give the command "Fetch." Touch the buck with the toe of your foot to suggest action and when he picks it up, back away, repeating the command "Fetch." When he brings it to you, praise and pet him. If he refuses, bring the yoke back into play again.

Soon he will catch the spirit of the work and hunt for the buck without assistance from you. When he finds the buck, do not allow him to carry it off, but, by means of the cord, force him to bring it to you immediately.

Force retrieving is taught in steps. Each step may require a different number of lessons, but never try to advance the dog's training until he has learned the present lesson thoroughly.

Some dogs take to retrieving lessons quickly and soon enter into the work in a spirit of playfulness. Do not discourage this playfulness, for it is of much value. The dog will soon tire of playing, and then force must be brought into use. Never work the pupil for long periods. Fifteen minutes a lesson is enough, and always stop, if possible, when the dog has done a good piece of work. One lesson a day will serve, but two short periods, one in the morning and one in the afternoon, produce faster progress. If the dog shows signs of tiring before the fifteen-minute period is up, stop then.

Remember to go slow. Force must be employed, but take no chances of spoiling the pupil. A kind degree of firmness coupled with an abundance of patience will win out in the end. Your object is to develop a retriever that will do his work promptly and willingly at command, and with a "tender mouth."

The Ear-pinch System

The steps in the ear-pinch system are the same as those in the Webster Price method. The only difference lies in the manner of forcing the dog. In this system the pain is inflicted by pinching the dog's ear between the thumb and forefinger. The dog's collar may be held in the remaining three fingers on the hand. This method does not allow as much control over the dog as the retrieving yoke. It has one advantage, however, in that the source of punishment is always at hand, and the dog can be reminded of his laxity in the field by simply pinching his ear. I prefer the retrieving yoke, for once a dog learns his lesson under this method, he seldom forgets it.

Chapter 13

THE USE OF CONTROLLED GAME

୧୨୧୨

SCARCITY of game, accompanied by the increasing diffi-
culty in locating suitable training grounds, has brought about
a number of changes in the bird-dog-training technique employed in a number of sections.

Not all of us have ready access to game-filled fields. In
some sections the open seasons are so short that the opportunities for training under natural conditions are decidedly
limited. Hence, many sportsmen are resorting to the practice
of giving their young pupils preliminary field lessons under
conditions that are more or less artificial, using pen-raised
game birds and non-game birds, such as pigeons and guinea
fowl.

The most satisfactory training results to be obtained
through the use of controlled game are with the so-called
quail call-back trap and pen-reared bobwhite quail.

This trap is made in rectangular boxlike form from strong
small-mesh woven wire. It can be made of any dimensions
that will afford comfortable quarters for twelve or more
quail and be easily transported. Carl Beattie, R.F.D., Fulton,
New York, can furnish detailed plans and full instructions
at $1.00 a copy. Several game farms manufacture these traps

commercially and furnish the birds to go with them. All three sides and the floor are of wire to make the trap vermin-proof. The trap should be covered at one end against the weather. At the other end, a door or gate is placed to afford an exit for the birds to be released, to allow the trainer space in which to catch the birds with a small net if he so desires and to provide entry for food and water.

A good many of these traps are made in double or two-story fashion. The birds to be released are kept in the lower compartment, while their call-back companions are housed above them. About two or three inches above the bottom on each long side, flush with the side and leading into the lower compartment, are round tunnels made of small-mesh wire which allow the released birds to gain entry into the trap.

The trap is transported to a suitable area. Several birds are removed by the trainer and "planted" or allowed to walk out of the trap and fly in any direction they desire. The trainer marks the flight. The birds will not go far, as they are not accustomed to liberty.

After an appropriate wait, to allow the released birds to settle down, the trainer works his young pupil into the area and endeavors to get him on point, handling him just as if he were working with wild native game. By watching the flights carefully, the trainer can get in several pieces of work on the same bird. However, he should not tax the endurance of his birds too much, as pen-reared birds are not as strong as wild ones. The birds should occasionally be rotated in releasing so that all get the exercise.

After his work is finished, the trainer retires from the area. When sufficient time has passed, the birds remaining in the trap will begin to miss their comrades and, as is the habit of quail, will start the gathering, rallying, or covey call.

The still frightened, but unharmed, released birds are now anxious for the company of their own kind and quickly respond, working their way back to the trap. They have been housed and fed in it for days, and it is the only home they know.

Several birds should always be left in the lower compartment so they can readily be seen by the returning quail. The releasers easily find the tunnel entrances, and in they go. They never seem to realize they could go out the same way.

In late afternoon the trainer returns to find all or most of his birds back home. He can then return the trap to headquarters or leave it overnight, closing the tunnel entrances with the wooden slides affixed above them to prevent the entry of destructive vermin. There may be a straggler or two still out, but if the trainer places the trap in the same spot the next day, he will probably recover them. Of course, some never return, reverting to the wild or falling victims to vermin, and this is the risk the trainer takes. But it is amazing how seductive the call of the bobwhite is to a lonesome and frightened fellow quail faced with a solitary night out.

I know one trainer who, several years ago, limited his training string to twelve Weimaraners. He worked these dogs almost exclusively on twelve quail out of his call-back trap. At the end of the season, he had twelve well-trained pupils— and twelve weary, but still hardy bobwhite quail!

The development of the call-back trap in fairly recent years has been the most important improvement in training equipment in the last century. It has been a boon to the professional and amateur trainer alike.

The trap is easy to build and inexpensive to buy, and with the widespread establishment of game farms throughout the country, quail are usually readily available in almost every community. Quail, at $1.00 to $1.50, are reasonably priced. With an investment of around $25.00 and permission to use a fairly open field or woodlot, any owner-trainer can provide himself with a ready-made training ground with the call-back trap. Of course, the birds must be fed, watered, and cared for, but this does not entail much trouble.

Releasing Traps

Through the years a number of traps have been introduced by which game and non-game birds can be held in semiconcealment and released at any time the trainer chooses. The traps have served a good purpose, but they have their drawbacks.

In order to put the birds in the traps, the birds must be handled. This imparts human scent to the birds, which causes the dog to realize all is not natural. This confuses him to some extent and reduces his enthusiasm. The problem can be minimized some by wearing gloves when handling the birds.

One of the best of these is the Stuart Trap, developed by Jack Stuart, the well-known professional trainer of Farwell, Michigan, and Stapleton, Alabama.

This trap will accommodate pheasant, quail, pigeons, etc. It allows the air to flow freely across the bird, so that the dog gets the full benefit of the bird scent.

A special feature is the fact that, holding the bird comfortably and unharmed, the trap, when sprung, tosses the bird in the air, thus insuring instant flight. The trap can be sprung from a distance by attaching a remote control cord. Full details can be obtained by writing Mr. Stuart.

Tethered Pheasants

The use of tethered birds is rather crude and is recommended only when the trainer does not want to employ other methods.

Probably the best results in training of this sort can be secured from the use of pheasants. These birds give off the proper type of scent, which will not easily become contaminated if care is exercised in handling them. Many sportsmen combine game restoration programs with bird-dog training and, after using the pheasants for a period of training, release them in favored gunning covers. The pheasants will come through the period of training unharmed if careful methods of handling are adopted.

Select a low meadow in which the grass is fairly high in spots. Attach a stout cord some four feet long to the leg of the pheasant. To this cord tie a stick of sufficient weight to prevent the bird from flying a long distance but light enough to allow him to make a flight of considerable length. In "planting" the bird, place it in a small clump of grass with some cover about, taking care to wear leather gloves in handling the bird to keep down scent adulteration. Cover the bird over lightly with grass. It will probably remain crouched in this clump for a considerable length of time, but if it should attempt to walk away, the stick will catch in the cover and prevent it. After the bird is settled in the grass clump, place the stick where it will aid you in locating the bird. Back away from the bird quietly.

Do not work the dog directly to the bird. Take a circuitous route, allowing him to range as usual, but gradually swinging around so that the wind will be right for him as he approaches the bird. When he points, handle him as usual. Presently, pick up the stick and allow the bird to flush. If you raise the stick and release it when the bird takes flight, you will eliminate the danger of the stick's becoming caught in the cover and jerking the bird to earth. Should the unexpected happen, however, you must be alert to handle your dog, for he will probably think the pheasant is crippled and dash forward to catch it. A clean flight is what you desire for best training results, for then temptation is diminished. If possible, get a companion to go along and flush the bird for you while you handle your dog.

Mark the bird down carefully. It cannot go far when it alights, as the stick will become caught in the cover. Then work the dog in another direction, gradually shaping your course to come in contact with the bird again. If care is exercised, several excellent pieces of work can be obtained on a single bird in one afternoon. The pheasant's physical endurance cannot be taxed too heavily, however, and after a few flights he should be returned to his crate and pen.

These birds can be employed in every department of field training, and contact with them will invariably serve to revive flagging interest on the part of the pupil. The same methods of procedure are to be followed as in training on native game.

Some exponents of the use of hand-reared pheasants put the birds "to sleep" when planting them. This is done by grasping the bird by the sides with both hands, swinging it a few moments with a circular motion, and then laying it on its side with its head tucked under the wing next the ground. This is good procedure to employ in releasing birds in field-trial bird fields, but it is not especially recommended for training, as the bird is powerless to escape should the young dog pounce upon it. Pheasants placed in this position will often remain motionless for long periods.

Guinea Fowl

This queer-looking fowl is really only semidomesticated in its habits and can rustle for itself in favorable environs. These birds give off what is apparently a gamy scent, and most dogs will point young broods of them stanchly. Many dogs, especially those that have been worked on these birds as puppies, will point adult guineas as well. It is on the young birds, however, that the best results can be obtained from aged dogs. A well-known professional in New England recently told me that he could secure just as good results from work on a flock of young guineas as he could from a brood of young ruffed grouse. The young birds do not need to be tethered but should merely be released in the covers hunted.

The adult guinea can be put to good use in developing the pointing instinct in puppies.

Tie a short, stout cord around the guinea's wings close to where they join the body, allowing the wings a little play. To this loop tie another stout cord six or seven feet long, which in turn is attached to a strong cane fishing pole. This will allow you to lift the fowl from the ground by its wings.

Plant the bird in the same fashion as recommended for the pheasant. Work the puppy up gradually toward the bird. After the puppy has established a point, handle him as usual, and have an assistant flush the bird in sight of the puppy by raising it off the ground with the pole. This is, of course, quite artificial, but it is surprising to see at what early ages some embryonic candidates for field honors will point these birds.

The guinea can also be tethered or hobbled as described for the pheasant, and it will sometimes fly good distances when flushed. These birds are quite hardy and often take considerable pummeling from young puppies without apparent damage.

Pigeons

The use of pigeons in off-season training is growing in popularity. These birds are inexpensive and easily kept, and they flush with vigor. They are especially valuable in correcting faults, such as shot breaking, and they can be employed to good advantage in making a dog steady to wing.

In using pigeons, it is best to secure a number of breeders of the homing variety and raise your own birds in your loft. In this way you will seldom lose one after it is released in the field. These birds are strong flyers and quite hardy. They give off a scent that bird dogs seem to like, and most dogs will point them with the same intensity as shown on game birds, provided they cannot see the pigeon.

Many old-time trainers used pigeons extensively, but the practice of using them has come into vogue among the younger generation to a notable extent only in recent years. I know several trainers who use these birds almost exclusively during most of the year simply because of the extreme scarcity of game, a problem that is becoming increasingly serious in many sections.

There are two methods of "staking" these birds. One is by using a small cage, the other by putting the bird's head under its wing and laying the bird on its side with this wing next the ground.

A trainer friend of the old school recommends the cage method highly, as he has used it for years. He says the scenting is better and, of course, the bird is protected from the dog. The smaller the cage the better, as this facilitates hiding it. It is made of one-fourth-inch mesh wire, with one end and the floor of wood. A good size is eight inches long, four inches wide, and five inches high. The door should be so hinged as to open down, allowing the bird to walk out on it to make his flight. The door should be equipped with an easily released catch or trigger on the top.

In planting the bird, the cage should be concealed well, lightly covered with grass. Too much grass, however, will interfere with the spread of the scent. Never work the dog directly up to the cage and never let him see it if this can be prevented. Let him range out in the usual way, gradually turning him toward the concealed cage. After you have secured a point, do not be in a hurry to flush the bird. Stamp around in the grass as if you were trying to kick up a game bird, then spring the door open, giving the cage a slight jar with the toe of the shoe. This will bring the pigeon out in a hurry, and his flight will be made in plain sight of the dog.

A number of caged birds can be placed about a field and the dog worked from one to another. The released pigeons fly back to the loft. If the dog refuses to point these birds at first, he can be encouraged to do so by bringing him up behind a pointing dog for a back and then allowing him to see the bird flushed. Lead him up and let him smell the cover in which the cage was placed, and he will soon begin to point them.

Another trainer friend, equally enthusiastic about the use of pigeons for training, derides the cage method as being too artificial. He says the cage is too hard to hide, the birds flutter around at the approach of the dog, the cage interferes with the scent, and, in general, better results can be obtained from his method.

He uses young three-quarter-grown birds almost entirely, because they are easier to handle and stay put better. His system calls for the "dizzying" of the bird a bit by swinging it around in a circular motion several times. The pigeon's head is then tucked under its wing, and the bird tipped upside down in just enough cover to hide it, or laid on its side with the head under it. He plants about four of these birds in a single field and then works his dog or brace of dogs through cover leading to the field, getting the "wire edge" off this way. When he gets his dogs on point he handles them and flushes the bird in the usual way. He generally takes a helper with him, and uses as many as twenty pigeons, which he raises himself, in a morning's workout. Some of these birds are shot over the dogs' points.

Continued training on these birds, after the dog is once well started in handling game, is not recommended. If he catches sight of the cage a few times he begins to realize that these are artificial conditions and loses interest.

This work, however, can be made to serve a good purpose if not overdone. It is a splendid way to give the young dog work under the gun when game is extremely scarce or in the off season. Even in good game country, these birds may be used to correct faults, for adult pigeons can be obtained at all times.

The best results, however, are to be obtained from native game birds under natural conditions. All the tethered, hand-reared game birds or "synthetic" game in the world cannot teach a dog the ways of the wily ruffed grouse, the fleet-footed pheasant, the easy-going woodcock, or the rocketing quail.

Chapter 14

BIRD-DOG FIELD TRIALS

❦

FIELD TRIALS are events wherein individual bird dogs are given the opportunity to display their field qualities in direct competition.

They serve a varied purpose. The primary object is the improvement of the bird-dog breeds through a more general dissemination of information concerning bloodlines and breeding procedure. This knowledge, so essential if future bird-dog generations are to measure up to the highest standards of field performance, can be best obtained through the avenue of public competition provided in field trials. Field-trial standards approach the ideal, and the history of progress in American bird-dog breeding is found in the annals of the sport.

The social side of a field trial is one of its most attractive features. The friendships formed are lasting. There is always a spirit of good fellowship and camaraderie, and there is no class distinction among the devotees of the sport. Every field trial is a gathering of high-class sportsmen and sportswomen on common ground and in a common interest, and no higher degree of sportsmanship is prevalent in any sport.

The sport provides a medium for the interchange of constructive thoughts and ideas concerning everything pertaining to the gun dog and, while the theories advanced may not always be in accord, the ensuing arguments are in the spirit of friendliness.

Field trials have always been, and are now recognized as, outstanding contributions to game restoration and conservation programs. Many game-management programs, beneficial to the entire countryside, have been launched on field-trial grounds, the resulting research proving of great value to wildlife resources in general.

The first public field trial in America was held at Memphis, Tenn., October 8, 1874. The winner was Knight, a black setter dog belonging to H. Clark Pritchett. The stake was sponsored by the Tennessee State Sportsmen's Association, and the judges were J. W. Burton and J. H. Acklen.

This organization sponsored the sport exclusively until 1877, when the Hampton, Iowa, trials were held. Since that time the growth of interest has been continuous. From 1880 to 1890, the sport recorded an average of six field trials annually, with 120 dogs competing. The interest soon spread to all sections of the country, and in the decade from 1920 to 1930 an average of 144 trials, with 369 stakes, was established. During this period, an average of 5,535 bird dogs of various breeds competed annually in field trials. Since that time the sport has grown by leaps and bounds, until now there are a number of annual events in practically every section of the country. It is safe to estimate that there are now far more than 10,000 canine competitors appearing before the field-trial fancy annually.

In the early days the judges reached their decisions through the point system. The scale of points used approximated the following: Nose, 30; pace and style, 20; backing,

10; breaking, 15; retrieving, 5; style and stanchness in pointing, 15; roading, 5; total, 100.

In 1879 the first heat system was adopted. Under this method, each dog that defeated his brace mate or competitor was carried into the next series until the final elimination was made and the winner declared. This system was found unsatisfactory as, in the drawing, it was possible for the two best dogs to be run together in the first heat, thereby penalizing one good dog to the profit of an inferior one. So what is known as the "spotting system" came into being, and it prevails today.

Under the spotting method, the judges are unhampered by red tape and unnecessary rules and are left free to pick the winners from the performances recorded. The contesting dogs are run in braces, the running time of the first-series heats being stipulated in the rules of the club. Unless the winners stand out decisively at the end of the first series, the dogs that have performed with the most brilliancy are picked as second-series contenders, braced in any manner the judges may desire, and put down again, running until the judges are satisfied as to the comparative merits of the contestants on that occasion.

The first-series heats in a field trial are all of the same duration, but the time allotted for second-series competition is at the direction of the judges unless otherwise stipulated in club rules.

With the increase in interest, it is only natural that there should be a number of changes in *modus operandi* of field trials. Now there are puppy stages of dogs up to certain age limits; derby events for candidates beyond thirty months of age; and all-age stakes open to all ages. There are amateur and professional stakes, winners' events, championship competitions, and shooting-dog stakes.

In the early days field-trial dogs were handled from afoot.

Changes in conditions, the scarcity of game, difference in standards have brought about an abandonment of this practice, and now practically everyone who attends a major field trial follows the running from horseback. Professional handlers train from horseback almost exclusively. This, of course, does not apply to the shooting-dog stakes or the cover-dog trials in grouse country, where the handlers,. and in some instances the judges, walk.

The so-called "big circuit" of major trials is composed of a series of clubs holding annual events in the prairie-chicken and quail sections. These are inaugurated annually on the Canadian prairies and continue through the winter months, generally closing with the National Championship held toward the end of winter. These trials are all held under natural conditions, the courses being laid out across country. The entrance and starting fees are comparatively high and the cash purses correspondingly large. The heats range from thirty minutes to three hours' duration.

When the curtain falls on the winter competition, the spring events are ushered in. These are generally held on one-course grounds in the East, with liberated birds providing the game.

The dogs that compete in the major stakes are considered the cream of the country, and it is upon their performances that the pendulum of breeding activity generally swings. Many of these dogs are developed for field-trial and stud purposes only, although a number of them are annually used by their owners in the season's shooting. The dogs of A. G. C. Sage, prominent New York sportsman, who has won more National Championships than any one individual owner, are developed along combination lines. Entered only in the fastest company, they are always dangerous competitors and are shot over each year by their owner at Sedgefields, his Alabama preserve. Other notable examples of field-trial shooting dogs are Sioux, Candy Kid, Feagan's Mohawk Pal, Doughboy, Becky Broomhill, Norias Roy, and Mississippi Zev. All were field-trial champions and all were excellent shooting dogs.

There has been, and always will be, extensive discussion of the ability of the dog developed for field trials to adapt himself to the requirements of shooting. Years ago this question formed the basis of an interesting competition between the famous sportsmen, Herman B. Duryea and Pierre Lorillard. Duryea selected J. M. Avent, the veteran professional handler who had charge of the Duryea string of field-trial dogs, as his shooting companion. Lorillard selected a companion and pitted the bird-finding ability of his shooting dogs against the Duryea field-trial winners. The competition was to be determined by the number of birds each party bagged on a given day.

Of course, marksmanship was an equation of the contest, but all were expert shots and no handicap was asked or given. The Duryea-Avent combination won by a wide margin, not only in the number of birds bagged, but also in the number of coveys and singles found and handled. The great setter bitch Double National Champion Sioux was a member of the Duryea-Avent string. She was hunted in short heats several times during the day and found more birds than any dog that competed.

There is no reason why the properly trained field-trial winner cannot be used to the best advantage as a shooting dog in the type of country in which he has been developed. The winning setter, Phil Essig, was a shooting dog of the finest quality, and the noted Eugene's Ghost, always difficult to handle in field-trial competition, was shot over heavily after his field-trial career was ended.

Several of the major clubs hold "owner-handler stakes" in which the competing dogs must be owned and handled by the owners. These events provide some interesting races, as a number of these dogs have been professionally trained and campaigned in major trials.

This brings up the question: Can an amateur develop and successfully campaign a dog in major field trials? The answer is: It has been done and is being done. Cecil S. Proctor, Oklahoma City fancier, Carl E. Duffield, Tyler, Texas, sportsman, and the late C. Watt Campbell, Tulsa, Okla., have won important stakes in open trials with dogs they have trained themselves. Both Proctor and Duffield have handled first-place winners in the American Field Futurity, the annual derby classic. Raymond B. Hoagland, Cartersville, Ga., Harry C. Kirkover, Aiken, S. C., George M. Rogers, Mt. Holly, N. J., the late Louis M Bobbitt, Winston-Salem, N. C., Dr. Alvin Nitchman, Cranbury, N. J., and Virgil P. Hawse, Staunton, Va., have all been frequent winners in open stakes with dogs they have trained themselves. In the New England cover-dog trials, Dr. James S. Goodwin, Concord, Mass., is a frequent winner with dogs of his own training.

. The amateur is, indeed, handicapped in competition with professionals. Bird-dog training with him is a hobby, a source of pleasant and healthful recreation. Consequently he cannot devote as much time to his dogs as the professional, who makes bird-dog training a business. The professional trainer is a valuable asset to the general bird-dog fraternity. He makes the sport possible for many enthusiasts who do not have the time or facilities to train their own dogs. He lives a hard life, his work returns comparatively little in a financial way, and he generally adopts his vocation as a life's work because of his love for bird dogs and the outdoors.

The amateur trials really constitute the backbone of the sport. In these events, the entries are generally made up from the ranks of shooting dogs and are handled, in the main, by their fond owners. The trophies given as prizes are highly prized, not so much for the intrinsic value, but as evidence of accomplishment. These trials are "feeders" for the major circuit, as many of the patrons of amateur events are ambitious to own and campaign a big-time contender. The premier amateur events of each year are the Regional Amateur Championships, and the National Quail and Pheasant Championships, sponsored by the Association of Amateur Field Trial Clubs of America.

The *American Field*, a weekly publication with headquarters in Chicago, devotes most of its editorial matter to field-trial activities and matters pertaining to the gun dog. The publication maintains the *Field Dog Stud Book* and sponsors the American Field Futurity (run on quail) and the American Field Pheasant Futurity, breeders' stakes staged annually.

Our advice to the novitiate in the field of bird-dog activities is to attend a few field trials. Ride the courses, see all the running, ask questions. They will provide an excellent medium for the comparison of the performance of your own dog with that of others. In attending these events you will meet genuine sportsmen always willing to extend a helping hand to a fellow fancier. These contacts will prove of value in the development of your own dog.

Acquaintanceships formed at field trials often ripen into long and valued friendships.

A list of important field trials and the winners of the various stakes through the years is contained in another chapter.

Chapter 15

TIPS ON DOG CARE

෨ඥ෨

THE AUTHOR of this book makes no pretense of being an expert or authority on diseases of dogs. We have always tried to practice the theory that the best cure is prevention, and prevention comes, in the main, from prompt attention to and correction of conditions that are obviously wrong. This, coupled with a constant war against worms and a rigid program of *cleanliness* around the kennel, accounts in the main, in my opinion, for the fact that my dogs are generally in pretty good condition and my veterinarian bills have been comparatively small. Frankly, I'm knocking on wood when I say that.

At the same time, I have never been a great believer in so-called home remedies or cure-alls. This is not to say that there are not good and effective patent medicines on the market. As a general rule, these products, when advertised in a reputable publication, are backed by much research and designed to do the job claimed for them. When I get in a jam, however, I don't reach for the first bottle on the shelf. I call on the services of a competent veterinarian—and pronto.

Some of us are not so located that competent veterinarians

who specialize in the treatment of canine diseases are close by. Consequently, we have to rely on what we read or what friends tell us.

Among my friends I am proud to number Mr. Edwin M. Berolzheimer, owner of the Cloister Kennels, which house what field-trial records prove to be the finest group of field-working Irish setters in the country. Extremely thorough in his every undertaking, from directing the affairs of the Eagle Pencil Company, of which he is part owner, to caring for his dogs, Mr. Berolzheimer has made a close study of canine ailments and diseases, and I know of no man, outside of the veterinarian profession, whose knowledge on these subjects is so profound. Much of the information contained in this chapter was gained from him. I know he speaks with authority and from personal experience.

Control of External Parasites

In the control of external parasites, such as fleas and ticks, Mr. Berolzheimer is a firm believer in derris powder. This powder contains varying amounts of rotonone, about 5 per cent in the average. Most of it comes from the East Indies, although some is imported from South America.

In sprinkling or dusting derris powder into the hair and skin, it should be mixed with talcum powder to such extent that the rotonone content is about 1 per cent. Two pounds of derris with eight pounds of talc is about right. Dust on with a spray gun and rub in. The dog should not be hunted for twenty-four hours after dusting, as the powder has a tendency to interfere with his nose to a small extent.

In using derris powder in a dip, dissolve one ounce of soap in one gallon of water, add two to four ounces of derris powder of which the rotonone content is 5 per cent. Derris powder can be purchased in that strength. It should be kept in a light-proof container, as its strength deteriorates rapidly in sunlight. Derris powder's effects will last longer in a dip than in the powdered form. It is a better summertime treatment. Don't wash it off.

About Distemper

Through the use of preventive inoculations, distemper, which for many years took disastrous annual toll from the ranks of gun dogs, no longer stands as the scourge of dogdom. We highly recommend the inoculation of every young dog against this disease. It has been truthfully said that "your dog is only half a dog until he has either had distemper or been inoculated against it." There are several effective methods on the market. All should be administered by a competent veterinarian, and his advice regarding them should be accepted.

According to Mr. Berolzheimer, there is only one true distemper. This disease is due to a filtrable virus that manifests itself in various forms with various symptoms. It is often confused with other diseases or ailments.

The real damage is done by the secondary invaders that come after about a week of distemper. The disease, in itself, is comparatively mild. Influenza is its nearest counterpart in human beings.

One of its main dangers is the fact that after about four days of high temperature the temperature drops to a flat normal, and the inexperienced owner begins to think his dog is out of danger. This is the real danger signal, however, and the time to take every precaution against a relapse.

Some of the symptoms are loss of appetite, discharge from the eyes and nose, coughing, rapid breathing, and rise in temperature. A thermometer is an indispensable instrument around a well-operated kennel, for temperature tells the story of a dog's condition many, many times.

At the first sign, or even suspicion, of distemper, serum should be given frequently, at least 100 cc. immediately to young bird dogs and hounds. Repeat this dose in twelve hours and then give the same every twenty-four hours for three or four days. This is given subcutaneously or intravenously by hypodermic. Mr. Berolzheimer advises the use of large doses of penicillin (50 to 100 thousand units at the first dose, then 25 to 50 thousand units every three hours, around the clock, so that the dog receives 200 to 400 thousand units per day). If penicillin is not used in large doses the bacteria may become resistant to the drug. It is generally unnecessary to use any drug except penicillin, but if there are no signs of improvement within forty-eight hours, it may also be necessary to use the sulfa drugs in addition.

Use one and one-half grains sulfadiazine and one and one-half grains sulfathiazole per pound body weight per day, divided into six doses, one dose every four hours. For a fifty-pound dog, the dosage should be 150 grains daily, 25 grains per dose, or one and one-half 7.7-grain tablets of each. With each dose give ten to fifteen grains of bicarbonate of soda. After twenty-four to forty-eight hours, this dose should be reduced to one grain of each sulfa drug per pound body weight per day.

If a dog reacts unfavorably to the sulfa drugs, stop using them. There will be no reaction to the penicillin.

Do not try to control the dog's temperature for twenty-four hours. After twenty-four hours, if the temperature is over 102, give one five-grain aspirin or one empirin tablet with five to ten grains of bicarbonate of soda every four hours. If the temperature is 103 or over, give two tablets. If it is 104 or over, give three tablets. Lessen the dose as the temperature drops.

For the cough that generally accompanies distemper, and is so obviously painful, give one-quarter grain of codeine with the aspirin every four hours.

If bacterial infections in the intestines, such as diarrhea, accompany the distemper, two 7.7-grain tablets of sulfasuxidine should be given every four hours.

Diarrhea

For diarrhea of any kind from any cause, the well-known fancier recommends the following: one tablespoonful kaolin and one teaspoonful of bismuth subcarbonate mixed with a little water, and five drops of deodorized tincture of opium Administer as often as every three hours until stools become normal, but not more than six doses a day.

Care of Eyes

Keep the eyes washed out with a solution of boric acid by mixing one teaspoonful to eight ounces of boiling water, strained through a clean handkerchief or cloth, then allow to cool. Flush eyes well to prevent ulceration. Also use sulfathiazole ophthalmic ointment or penicillin ophthalmic ointment (latter must be kept in refrigerator).

Feeding

Nursing plays a great part in the successful treatment of distemper or any other disease, for that matter, and food is absolutely essential to keep up sufficient strength to combat the ailment. If the dog refuses food for twenty-four hours, he should be force fed. This is particularly true in distemper cases.

A nourishing meal for sick dogs can be made by preparing

a gruel in the following manner: Make sixteen ounces of soup as follows; mix four ounces of Karo syrup and two soft-boiled eggs (two minutes) with ten ounces of homemade chicken or beef broth. Take four tablespoonfuls or two ounces of this, saving the balance in the refrigerator, and mix with five ounces of cooked cereal or Pablum made with milk, and one ounce of chopped beef, a total of eight ounces. This should make an extremely thick gruel. Put some of it in a small wine or medicine glass and pour it slowly into the corner of the dog's mouth, by inserting the finger of your left hand between the corner of the lips and the teeth and holding the lips away. Wait until the dog has swallowed before pouring more, so that he will not choke. Don't give too much at one time, or it will make the dog vomit. However, try to feed at least four times a day. If the dog begins to struggle, reduce feedings to four ounces and give eight times a day.

If the sick dog continues to have an appetite, however, feed him anything he will take, as much meat as possible. A tempting and nourishing (although it doesn't sound so) meal can be made by boiling chicken heads and feet to the consistency of a soft jelly. Barely cover with water and cook for three quarters of an hour, adding water as needed.

Keep the dog off the floor in a room with the temperature at seventy degrees. Give him plenty of fresh air but prevent all drafts.

Worming

Mr. Berolzheimer recommends worming puppies at an early age. He suggests a microscopic examination of the stools at five weeks of age. The chances are ninety-nine out of one hundred that round worms will be present. If round worms are found, the puppies should be wormed at six weeks of age, using one-tenth of a cc. per pound weight of tetrachloroethylene. Feed the usual meal the night before. Worm them in the

morning on empty stomachs. Two hours later give one teaspoonful to one tablespoonful of milk of magnesia. One hour
later give them soup and cereal. Then resume regular feeding.

Their stools should be checked for worms occasionally. As
the puppies grow larger and the amount of the vermifuge is
increased, the amount of the milk of magnesia should also be
increased. For twenty-four hours prior to and four hours after
dosing, give no fats, cream, milk, or oily food. Young dogs
should be wormed every six months.

For tapeworms, Mr. Berolzheimer recommends Nemural,
the trade name for Winthrop Chemical Company's drocarbil.
Feed light meal with some milk in the morning. Two hours
later give tablets in the following dosage: one tablet for every
pound body weight, except in case of aged dogs, when the
dose should be one tablet for every fifteen pounds body
weight. Give three tablespoonfuls castor oil one and one-half
hours later. Bowels should move in from fifteen minutes to
one hour. If the dog has severe cramps, give one one-
hundredth grain of atropin sulphate. Repeat worming in ten
to fourteen days.

Hook and Whipworms

For hookworms the same dosage of tetrachloroethylene as
for roundworms is also effective, but until the discovery of
N-Butyl Chloride (trade name Bu-Chlorin) there was no
effective treatment for whipworms, except removing the
secum. N-Butyl Chloride is also quite effective against round
and hookworms and is much less toxic than tetrachloroethylene.

Dose for a fifty-pound dog is one five-cc. capsule for round
and hookworms and five five-cc. capsules (25 cc.'s) for whipworms after fasting eighteen to twenty-four hours. Follow in
an hour with one and one-half ounces castor oil, and two
hours later give warm soup or milk. For whipworms, the

worming should be repeated one to three times with ten to fourteen day intervals

Heart Worms

One of the great scourges of the dog world today is heart worm, technically known as dirofilaria inmitis.

It is extremely important to have the dog's blood examined under a microscope every six months by a competent veterinarian because, if discovered at an early stage, the large majority of cases can be cured quite satisfactorily.

The microscopic young worm is transmitted from one dog to another by mosquitoes and perhaps other external parasites, and finally lands in the heart, where it grows to about ten inches in length with the diameter of the lead of a pencil. The dog that is heavily infected tires very rapidly and has a hacking cough. But when these symptoms are seen, the dog may be too far advanced for treatment, and that is why it is so important to make periodic microscopic examinations.

The present treatment is the intramuscular or intravenous injection of Fouadin. Since World War II, because some of our soldiers became infested with a similar disease prevalent in the tropics, a great deal of research has been done with other drugs, and it is hoped that an even more effective drug than Fouadin will soon be on the market. The drug should be administered by a competent veterinarian who has had experience in the treatment of heart worm.

Ear Canker

Ear canker is a troublesome ailment that gives the dog much discomfort. It is generally caused from moisture in the ear. The ear should be cleaned carefully and gently, using a cotton swab dipped in ether. Then apply zinc ointment generously with the swab. Do this daily until the ear improves, then every three or four days. Also powder with a composition of the following: bismuth oxyiodide 3 per cent, thymol iodide 15 per cent, boric acid 82 per cent.

Skin Eruptions

An excellent salve for skin eruptions or scratches is made of the following: sublimated sulphur 4 per cent, salicylic acid 3 per cent, bismuth subgallate 5 per cent, ichthyol 4 per cent, balsam of Peru 4 per cent, glycerine 2 per cent, and white vaseline and lanolin in equal parts to make 100 per cent.

Black Tongue

Black tongue, says Mr. Berolzheimer, is practically the same as pellagra in man. It is due to malnutrition and lack of niacin, the nicotinic acid that is contained in liver, meat, and yeast. The disease is generally found in dogs that eat large quantities of corn meal and little else. Corn meal contains a factor that interferes with the ultilization of niacin. Symptoms are: The mouth, gums, and tongue become very red; the dog salivates, loses appetite, has bloody diarrhea, ulcerations of the mouth, and foul breath odor. Finally the tongue become necrotic and gangrenous.

The treatment consists of 100 to 200 units of nicotinic acid daily, liver injections, and large doses of Vitamin B complex. Feed practically nothing but meat and liver.

Fright Disease

Fright disease is commonly called "running fits." The dog acts crazily, running in circles, barking or howling, etc., generally after violent exercise or upon becoming excited.

Get your hands on him as soon as possible, holding him down, and trying to soothe him. The treatment: one five-grain tablet of mercurochrome three times daily for a week. Put him on a raw-meat diet, little else. Don't become alarmed if his stools are red. This is caused by the mercurochrome.

Rabies

The practice of vaccinating against rabies is a controversial subject. Mr. Berolzheimer contends that it can't do any harm and recommends it. He also recommends a second injection of rabies vaccine two weeks following the first and a single booster injection annually.

Mr. Berolzheimer, of course, has made an intensive study of the care of dogs and he puts his knowledge into practice. He realizes, also, that the average sporting-dog owner has neither his knowledge nor his equipment, but he feels that many of the common ailments in dogs could be prevented if only a little extra effort and time are taken to ensure proper diet and living conditions for them. "Know your symptoms before you begin treatment. Don't jump to conclusions. When in doubt, consult a competent veterinarian," is his sound advice.

GLOSSARY OF TERMS

Adaptability: That quality which enables a dog to conform intelligently his speed and range to various types of terrain and cover.

Action: The manner in which the dog moves, or travels, in the field.

All age: A dog that is over thirty months of age.

Attitude: The posture of the dog on point. Attitude can be lofty or low, intense or relaxed.

Backcast: A cast on which the dog works to the rear of the handler.

Backing: Coming to a point or stop upon sight of another dog pointing or standing still.

Belton: A type of color formed when two colors blend so closely as to lose individual identity. Blue belton is a combination of black and white; orange belton a combination of orange and white.

Bevy: A group of game birds, generally a brood, such as quail.

Body scent: The scent emanating from the bodies of game birds.

Bird dog: One bred for the purpose of hunting upland game birds. In this book the term has reference to the pointing breeds.

Birds: In this book the term refers to game birds, i.e., quail, pheasant, ruffed grouse, woodcock, and prairie chicken.

Bitch: A female dog.

Blinker: A term commonly used to denote a dog that points game and then leaves it before the flush, finds game and leaves it without point-

	ing or flushing, or points game and leaves it upon the approach of his handler.
Boldness:	Aggressiveness in hunting. Willingness to cast good distances from his handler if good cover invites. Willingness to breast heavy cover or rough going.
Bolter:	A dog that refuses to handle to the course prescribed by the handler. One that goes hunting in any direction he desires and refuses to obey his master's commands or signals.
Brace mate:	When dogs are worked in pairs, each is called the brace mate of the other.
Breaking shot:	When the dog breaks his point and dashes in when the shot is fired.
Breeding:	The ancestry of the dog.
Breeds:	Races or varieties of animals.
Broken:	Common expression to describe a finished performer. When a dog is thoroughly trained he is called "broken."
Buck:	An accessory used in teaching retrieving.
Bump:	Slang definition of a flush.
Cast:	A reaching out in search of game. When a dog is traveling toward an objective he is said to be "on a cast."
Caution:	A warning given to the dog.
Chasing:	When a dog dashes after the birds when they are flushed. Unsteadiness to flush.
Check cord:	A training appliance that is attached to the dog's collar.
Choke collar:	A collar made in the form of a noose, for the purpose of applying force in a humane manner.
Class:	A term denoting high quality of performance
Coat:	The dog's hair.

Cold-blooded: A pointing dog of unknown or unpedigreed ancestry.

Condition: The state of physical well-being.

Course: The territory to be covered in the hunt.

Cover: Vegetation. A certain area of wooded land to be hunted.

Cover dog: Generally refers to a dog that covers a close range.

Covey: A group of game birds, generally a brood, such as quail. A bevy.

Cramp: To force a dog's training, causing him to lose some of his boldness or aggressiveness.

Crossbreed: Denotes mixed ancestry, as a cross between two setter breeds.

Cutting back: A dog that casts back toward his handler seeking direction after completing a cast, instead of taking the signal or command at the end of it, is said to be cutting back.

Dash: Enthusiasm, spirit, quickness in action.

Derby: A dog more than eighteen months and less than thirty months old.

Dog: A male dog.

Dropper: A dog crossed between a pointer and a setter.

Drop to shot: When the dog drops to the ground as the shot is fired.

Drop to wing: Dropping to the ground as the birds are flushed.

Drawing: The process of moving up to locate game. Roading.

Eligible: The dog is eligible to registration in the various stud books when he comes from registered ancestry or possesses a certified pedigree.

False pointer: A dog that frequently points unproductively.

Feather:	The long hair on the setter's legs. Also to show signs of game scent.
Finished:	Thoroughly trained. Broken.
Fire:	Dash, enthusiasm, spirit.
Flag:	The long hair on the setter's tail.
Fling:	Generally a period of aimless running before the enthusiastic dog settles to hunting.
Flush:	To cause the game birds to fly. The rise of game birds.
Flushing wild:	The rise of game birds that have not been disturbed.
Foot scent:	The scent emanating from the feet of game birds.
Gait:	The manner of running or galloping.
Game:	Game birds.
Ground work:	The manner in which a dog hunts a given area, irrespective of game found.
Gun dog:	A trained dog of the pointing breeds that is used by sportsmen when gunning.
Gun-shy:	Fear of the report or sight of the gun.
Hacked:	The term describing a dog that is forced to hunt close to the gunner and is not allowed to range wide.
Hardheaded:	Headstrong. Hard to control.
Hard-mouthed:	A dog that chews or crushes his birds when retrieving is said to be hard-mouthed.
Handling:	The dog's response to the trainer's commands, signals, and directions.
Heat:	The length of the period in which the dog is hunted in training or field trials.
Heel, to:	When a dog walks quietly by the side or at the heels of the trainer.
Hunting:	Searching for game.

Indecisive point:	One in which positiveness is lacking.
Kennel:	The home of the dog.
Kennel breaker:	Dog that attempts to escape from his kennel.
Lay:	In reference to game birds, the act of remaining still.
Lead:	To cause the dog to follow under restraint. A cord, leather strap, or chain attached to the dog's collar by which he can be restrained.
Line-running:	Casting in straight lines rather than hunting all the birdy places.
Loftiness:	The quality of high action in the field or high attitude on point.
Manners:	The actions of the dog on point and at the flush and shot. The thoroughly broken dog displays "perfect manners."
Markings:	Spots or patches of color on the dog's body.
Meat dog:	A term generally applied to the slow, methodical plodder that can find and handle birds, but whose work does not approach brilliancy.
Mechanical dog:	One that has been placed under such restraint in training that he has become entirely dependent upon the handler for instructions, or that quarters the ground in the same methodical way always.
Merry:	Quick, snappy, lively, attractive.
Natural instincts:	Those inborn qualities characteristic to the bird dog, such as the desire to hunt and the instinct to point.
Nose:	The ability to smell game birds.
Obedience:	Quick response to the trainer's commands.
Pace:	The rate of speed at which the dog hunts.
Point:	A motionless pose assumed by the dog and indicating the proximity of game.

Potterer: The dog that spends a good deal of time on foot scent or in nosing about where birds have been, or is unable to distinguish between old and fresh scent, is called a potterer.

Plug shooting dog: One whose manners are acceptable but whose performance fails to measure up to high standards.

Prospect: An untrained dog that shows promise.

Puppy: A dog is known as a puppy until it reaches the age of eighteen months.

Quartering: The act of ranging back and forth across the course.

Range: The distance a dog hunts from his handler.

Refusal to back: When a dog ignores the brace-mate's point or refuses to stop until the scent of game registers in his own nostrils.

Registration: The record of the dog's ancestry in a recognized stud book.

Retrieving: When a dog brings an object back to the handler. Generally applied to the finding and fetching of dead or wounded game birds.

Roading: Moving up slowly to locate game. Drawing. Exercising the dog by leading him upon the road, highway, or across country.

Self-hunting: The dog that habitually leaves his master or kennel to go hunting without direction is called a self-hunter. The dog that ignores his master's directions and hunts the course in his own manner or leaves the course entirely to go hunting by himself is also termed a self-hunter.

Shot breaker: A dog that dashes in when the shot is fired.

Side-stepping: A form of blinking. When a dog finds birds but passes them by without pointing or flushing.

Sloppiness: Lack of intensity.

Sluggish: Latent. Slow in developing.

Spaying: Removing or extirpating the ovaries of a bitch.

Speed: Rate of motion.

Spike collar: A nooselike training collar with small spikes next to the dog's flesh.

Spirit: Enthusiasm, boldness, dash.

Stale: Overworked.

Stamina: Endurance.

Stanch: The word has reference to the dog's actions while pointing. The dog that will establish a point and hold it, without caution or admonition, until his handler flushes the birds may be regarded as stanch.

Steady: The word has reference to the dog's actions *after* the birds are flushed. The dog is steady to shot and wing when he retains his position after the birds are flushed and the shot is fired.

Stride: The leap of the dog while running.

Stud book: A publication in which the ancestry of the dog may be recorded.

Style: A term referring to the dog's general appearance when hunting or on point.

Swing, to: To turn the dog in the desired direction when hunting.

Trailing: The dog that continually follows his brace mate is called a trailer. One that continues to cast in front of his brace mate and challenge him to a race is called a "head-on trailer." A dog may also trail birds by foot scent.

Turning to whistle: Breaking the cast and swinging in response to the trainer's whistle.

Type: The dog that measures up to the standards established for bird-dog conformation may be said to possess good type.

Wild flush: The rise of game birds for no apparent reason.

Yard breaking: That part of the dog's training given him in the yard.

IMPORTANT FIELD-TRIAL RECORDS

WINNERS IN THE AMERICAN FIELD QUAIL FUTURITY

Year	Name	Breed and Sex	Sire	Dam	Owner	Handler
1905	Tonopaugh	SD	Tony Boy	Sport's Estell	W. T. Hunter	Jake Bishop
1906	Lakefield Gleam	SD	Sport Count Danstone	Destiny's Princess	Lakefield Kennels	D. C. White
1907	Prince Rodney's Count	SD	Prince Rodney	Destiny's Lady	P. T. Schauf	Max Middleton
1908	Master John	SD	Count Whitestone	Marian Mills	H. R. Edwards	J. A. Gude
1909	Master Ben	SD	Marse Ben	Oktibbena	L. T. Cheek	W. D. Gilchrist
1910	Master Devereux	SD	Count Whitestone	Ora	H. R. Edwards	G. T. Dozier
1911	La Besita	SB	Count Whitestone	El Beso	F. M. Stephenson	W. H. Beazell
1912	Sadie G	SB	Jay R Whitestone	Krueger's Pride	J. A. Gude	J. A. Gude
1913	Louisiana Duke	PD	Fishel's Frank	King's Sister	J. J. Smith	Herbert Fishel
1914	Jay R's Boy	SD	Jay R Whitestone	Trixie Danstone	Dr. T. H. Clark	J. A. Gude
1915	Gunner	SD	Free Lance	Cotton Blossom	U. M. Fleischmann & F. T. Bedford	C. H. Babcock
1916	Little Boy Blue	SD	Noble Freelance	Becky Mohawk's Mischief	J. R. MacMillan	J. A. Gude
1917	Great Island Ringing Bells	PB	Tom Speedy	Lorna Doone	William Ziegler Jr.	R. K. Armstrong
1918	Cincinnati Nat	PD	Frank's Den	Cincinnati Queen	H. F. Fellows	E. D. Garr
1919	Montpelier Yank	SD	McCoy's King	Eugenia Maid	Miss M. DuPont	R. K. Armstrong
1920	Brookfield Kid	SD	Candy Kid	La Tisba	C. E. Duffield	C. E. Duffield
1921	Belle of Joyeuse	SB	Momoney	Princess Lou Rodney	J. K. Ottley	Ed Farrior
1922	Miss Joy Ferris	PB	Ferris' Manitoba Rap	Blue Streak	G. B. Robertson	Ed Farrior
1923	Warman's Lady	SB	Montpelier Man O'War	Sportess	C. E. Duffield	C. H. Harris
1924	White Cloth	PB	Comanche Zig Field	Burger's Johanna	J. C. Foster Jr.	M. R. Pritchette
1925	Arkansas	PD	Prairie Jack	Frank's Madge	F. R. Billingslea	Mack Pritchette

Year	Dog				Owner	
1926	Superlette	PB	Milligan's Dan	Doughboy's Kelona Lady	A. G. C. Sage	J. L. Holloway
1927	Lolo's Mr. Gibson	PD	Lolo's Hoot Gibson	Collinsville Beauty	Mrs. Lolo Kirkpatrick	Lon Kirkpatrick
1928	Muscle Shoals Sam	SD	Muscle Shoals' Jake	Sue Tate	Proctor & Tate	C. S. Proctor
1929	Outacite	PD	Gentleman Ginger	Speedstone's Traveler	C. V. La Dow	M. E. McMichael
1930	Sinco	PD	Muscle Shoals' Jake	Outcast	H. M. Balch	Pete Dixon
1931	Gangster	PB	John Willing Jr.	Myers Ruth	Emmy Haggin	Prather Robinson
1932	Spunky Creek Crook	PD	Catoosa Bob	Spunky Creek Flash	Mrs. F. R. Billingslea	Mack Pritchette
1933	Norias Esso	PD	Norias Roy	Myers Ruth	W. C. Teagle	Prather Robinson
1934	Worry Wart	PB	Kremlin	Myers Ruth	Jacob France	Prather Robinson
1935	Maryland Louise	PB	Norias Roy	Forest Flower	Jacob France	C. H. Harris
1936	Nola	PB	Ichaway	Doone's Frosty Midge	R. L. Jones	T. M. Lunsford
1937	Morpheus	PD	Joe Willing	Lullaby	A. G. C. Sage	Clyde Morton
1938	Luminary	PD	Doctor Blue Willing	Lullaby	A. G. C. Sage	Clyde Morton
1939	Ariel	PD	Air Pilot's Sam	Lullaby	A. G. C. Sage	Clyde Morton
1940	Dreamy	PB	Morpheus	Sedgefields Chiquita	A. G. C. Sage	Clyde Morton
1941	Astra	PB	Luminary	Tarantella	A. G. C. Sage	Clyde Morton
1942	Norias Burke	PB	Ichauway's Mike	Norias Mattie	W. C. Teagle	C. H. Harris
1943	Bonsoir	PD	Nightcap	Rockabye Baby	A. G. C. Sage	Clyde Morton
1944	Oration	PD	Homerun Harrigan	Flying Girl	A. G. C. Sage	Clyde Morton
1945	Bolero	PD	Nightcap	Tarantella	A. G. C. Sage	Clyde Morton
1946	Pandemonium	PD	Homerun Harrigan	Flying Girl	A. G. C. Sage	Clyde Morton
1947	Tennessee Zev	SD	Mississippi Zev	Mohawk's Peerless Kate	W. L. Nichol	J. Earl Bufkin
1948	Kilsyth Forshalee Rocky	PD	Darby's Tip	Forshalee Kay's Kate	Mrs. G. M. Livingston	G. A. Evans
1949	Fast Air Delivery	PD	Fast Delivery	Delivery Boy's Girl	A. B. Bobbitt	Paul Walker
1950	Satilla Wahoo Pete	PD	Satilla Sam	Fisher's Wahoo Mary	Leonard Waldron	J. S. Gates
1951	Kilsyth Dynamite Goodloe	PD	Shore's Brownie Doone	Kilsyth Delivery Dot	Mrs. G. M. Livingston	G. A. Evans
1952	Crafty	PD	Knockdown	Weiser's Winnie	John H. Gardner	John H. Gardner
1953	Storm Trooper	PD	Stormy Mike	Bettie Shanks	B. McCall	Frank Dimke
1954	Fast Delivery Belle	PB	Fast Delivery	Nightcap Girl	Miss Murtis L. Carver	Paul Walker
1955	John Storm	PD	Stormy Mike	Dandy Bow	B. McCall	Ed Farrior
1956	Warhoop Storm	PD	Warhoop Jake	Storm's Kate	B. McCall	Ed Farrior
1957	Dixie Melody	PD	Satilla Wahoo Pete	Drug Package	H. E. Weil	John S. Gates
1958	Medallion II	PD	Medallion	Stanton's June	Dr. W. B. Griffin	John S. Gates
1959	Gunsmoke's Jewel	PB	Gunsmoke	Santee Susan	Dr. T. J. Lattimore	John S. Gates
1960	Riggins White Knight	PD	Major Ludington Boy	Stanley's Candy	R. W. Riggins	D. Hoyle Eaton

Year	Name	Breed and Sex	Sire	Dam	Owner	Handler
1961	Gunsmoke's Y on Way	PB	Gunsmoke	Titanup's Windy Way	J. D. Bayler	Howard Kirk
1962	War Exterminator	PD	War Storm	Sugarplum	C. C. Coon	John S. Gates
1963	Fast Jake Delivery	PD	Fast Drug Delivery	Renfro Delivery Girl	A. B. Bobbitt	Paul Walker
1964	Doctor's Stormy Mack	PD	Storm's Romance	Doug's Pepper	Dr. D. E. Hawthorne	E. B. Epperson
1965	Stuart's Rambling Rebel	PD	Rambling Rebel Dan	Deep Run Dot	Guy H. Lewis	Fred Arant Jr.
1966	Homerun Jim	PD	Homerun Johnny	Homerun Sis	Walter H. Wimmer	Fred Arant Jr.
1967	Oklahoma Flush	PD	Paladin's Royal Flush	Baconrind's Sandy	Dr. I. J. Hammond	J. R. Gates

WINNERS OF THE NATIONAL BIRD DOG CHAMPIONSHIP

Year	Name	Breed and Sex	Sire	Dam	Owner	Handler
1896	Count Gladstone IV	SD	Count Noble	Ruby's Girl	Avent and Hitchcock	J. M. Avent
1898	Tony's Gale	SD	Antonio	Nellie G	Eldred Kennels	D. E. Rose
1899	Joe Cumming	SD	Antonio	Picciola	W. W. Titus	W. W. Titus
1900	Lady's Count Gladstone	SD	Count Gladstone IV	Dan's Lady	G. G. Williamson	D. E. Rose
1901	Sioux	SB	Count Gladstone IV	Hester Prynne	Avent and Duryea	J. M. Avent
1902	Sioux	SB	Count Gladstone IV	Hester Prynne	Avent and Duryea	J. M. Avent
1903	Geneva	SB	Tony Boy	Lena Belle	Pierre Lorillard	Charles Tucker
1904	Mohawk II	SD	Tony Boy	Countess Meteor	Avent and Duryea	J. M. Avent
1905	Alambagh	SD	Dash Antonio	Eldred Lark	Hobart Ames	C. E. Buckle
1906	Pioneer	SD	Count Whitestone	Bonnie Doone	G. N. Clemson	E. Shelley
1907	Prince Whitestone	SD	Count Whitestone	Queen Lilla	T. T. Pace	T. T. Pace
1908	Count Whitestone II	SD	Count Whitestone	Mecca's Lady	Dr. H. B. McMaster	E. D. Garr
1909	Manitoba Rap	PD	Ripple	Lady Cyrano Rush	Thomas Johnson	C. H. Babcock
1910	Monora	SB	Mohawk II	Tankas	J. M. Avent	J. M. Avent
1911	Eugene M	SD	Rosco Gladstone	Irene Cooper	Frank Reily	W. H. Elliott
1912	Commissioner	SD	Count Whitestone	Flossie May Fly	W. R. Craig	J. M. Avent
1913	Phillipides	SD	Prince Rodney	Mary Tudor	Fred S. Hall	J. A. Gude
1914	Comanche Frank	PD	Fishel's Frank	Lady Johns	U. R. Fishel	J. M. Avent
1915	La Besita	SB	Count Whitestone	El Beso	F. M. Stephenson	W. H. Beazell
1916	John Proctor	PD	Fishel's Frank	Miss Mariutch	A. L. Curtis	C. H. Babcock

Year	Winner		Sire	Dam	Owner	Breeder
1917	Mary Montrose	PB	Comanche Frank	Lorna Doone	William Ziegler Jr.	R. K. Armstrong
1918	Joe Muncie	SD	Jack Muncie	Miss Mathews	Benjamin Weil	J. M. Avent
1919	Mary Montrose	PB	Comanche Frank	Lorna Doone	William Ziegler Jr.	H. A. Tomlinson
1920	Mary Montrose	PB	Comanche Frank	Lorna Doone	William Ziegler Jr.	H. A. Tomlinson
1921	Ferris' Jake	PD	John Proctor	Lady Ferris	C. F. Griffith	Mack Pritchette
1922	Becky Broom Hill	PB	Broom Hill Dan	Nell's Queen Cott	L. L. Haggin	Chesley Harris
1923	Becky Broom Hill	PB	Broom Hill Dan	Nell's Queen Cott	L. L. Haggin	Chesley Harris
1924	Doughboy	PD	Nicholas Spettel	Kelona Lady	E. J. Rowe	J. W. Martin
1925	Becky Broom Hill	PB	Broom Hill Dan	Nell's Queen Cott	L. L. Haggin	Chesley Harris
1926	Feagin's Mohawk Pal	SD	Molemon	Mary Jepp	E. M. Tutwiler	Forrest Dean
1927	McTyre	PD	Milligan's Dan	McPherson's Choice	Jacob France	Chesley Harris
1928	Feagin's Mohawk Pal	SD	Molemon	Mary Jepp	E. M. Tutwiler Jr.	Forrest Dean
1929	Mary Blue	PB	James Ben Hur	Lee's Grace	W. C. Teagle	Chesley Harris
1930	Feagin's Mohawk Pal	SD	Molemon	Mary Jepp	E. M. Tutwiler Jr.	Forrest Dean
1931	Mary Blue	PB	James Ben Hur	Lee's Grace	W. C. Teagle	Chesley Harris
1932	Susquehanna Tom	PD	Highland Boy	Rap's Joy	Lebanon Kennels	Jake Bishop
1933	Rapid Transit	PD	The Hottentot	Milligan's Jane	A. G. C. Sage	Clyde Morton
1934	Norias Annie	PB	John Willing Jr.	Ben Hur's Countess	W. C. Teagle	C. H. Harris
1935	Homewood Flirtatious	PB	Seaview Rex	Wilder's Orange Lady	Homewood Kennels	F. E. Bevan
1936	Sulu	PB	The Hottentot	Lue's Sue	A. G. C. Sage	Clyde Morton
1937	Air Pilot's Sam	PD	Air Pilot	Nancy F	Ed Farrior	Ed Farrior
1939	Sport's Peerless Pride	SD	Sport's Peerless	Gore's Blue Bonnie	L. M. Bobbitt	W. D. English
1940	Lester's Enjoy's Wahoo	PD	Enjoy	Lester's Mary Lou	Dr. B. S. Lester	John S. Gates
1941	Ariel	PD	Air Pilot's Sam	Lullaby	A. G. C. Sage	Clyde Morton
1942	Luminary	PD	Doctor Blue Willing	Lullaby	A. G. C. Sage	Clyde Morton
1943	Ariel	PD	Air Pilot's Sam	Lullaby	A. G. C. Sage	Clyde Morton
1945	Ariel	PD	Air Pilot's Sam	Lullaby	A. G. C. Sage	Clyde Morton
1946	Mississippi Zev	SD	Peerless Eugene M	Red Flapper	Dr. W. R. Trapp	J. E. Bufkin
1947	Saturn	PD	Luminary	Hostess	A. G. C. Sage	Clyde Morton
1948	Peter Rinski	PD	Tennessee Dare Devil	Lady Willing Lady	R. R. Waugh	Ray Smith
1949	Sierra Joan	PB	Air Pilot Sammy	Titan's Girl	H. E. McGonigal	Howard Kirk
1950	Shore's Brownie Doone	PD	Claussen's Ranger Doone	Devotion's Kate	G. M. Livingston	G. A. Evans Jr.
1951	Paladin	PD	Ariel	Titan's Girl	A. G. C. Sage	Clyde Morton
1952	Paladin	PD	Ariel	Titan's Girl	Estate of A. G. C. Sage	Clyde Morton
1953	Shore's Brownie Doone	PD	Claussen's Ranger Doone	Devotion's Kate	Mrs. G. M. Livingston	George A. Evans
1954	Warhoop Jake	PD	Lester's Enjoy's Wahoo	Spunky Willing Diane	Dr. H. E. Longsdorf	Ed Mack Farrior
1955	Lone Survivor	PD	Luminary	Titanette	Dr. E. R. Calame	Leon Covington

WINNERS OF THE NATIONAL PHEASANT CHAMPIONSHIP

Year	Name	Breed and Sex	Sire	Dam	Owner	Handler
1926	Dan Woolton's Dauntless	PD	Cole's Dan Woolton	Iuka Bess	John Dunn	Curtis Thompson
1927	Village Girl	PB	Ferris' Manitoba Rap	Mary Winola	H. K. Crandall	H. K. Crandall
1928	Griffith's Happy Rap*	PD	Mount Riga Rap	Guynella	John Dunn	Curtis Thompson
1929	Rumson Farm Marex	PB	Seaview Rex	Rumson Farm Mary	Rumson Farm Ken	C. S. Ridge
1930	Schoolfield	PD	Tip of Joyeuse	Appalachian Mary	Gaines & Ruffin	Luther Smith
1931	Village Boy	PD	Seaview Rex	Village Girl	H. K. Crandall	Glenn Davis
1932	Village Boy	PD	Seaview Rex	Village Girl	H. K. Crandall	Glenn Davis
1933	Village Scout*	PD	Seaview Rex	Village Girl	F. A. Miller	E. A. Higgins
1934	Doctor Blue Willing	PD	Doctor Norman	Miss Willing	L. D. Johnson	Ed. Farrior
1935	Tip's Manitoba Jake*	PD	Bristol's Manitoba Rap	Muscle Shoals Betty	Mrs. E. H. Vare, Jr.	W. D. English
1936	Farmwood Yankee	PD	Yankee Doodle Jack	Farmwood Lou	U. M. Fleischmann	Sam O. Yount
1937	Lawless Boy	PD	Village Boy	Lawless Lady	Dr. H. E. Longsdorf	W. D. English
1956	Palamonium	PD	Paladin	Pandemonium's Dianah	Jimmy Hinton	Clyde Morton
1957	Wayriel Allegheny Sport	PD	Wayriel Jack	Allegheny Shendon Brownie	R. W. Riggins and Dr. J. A. Bays	Herman Smith
1958	The Arkansas Ranger	PD	Running W Wrangler	Ranger Bows	M. F. Mitchell	Jack Harper
1959	Palamonium	PD	Paladin	Pandemonium's Dianah	Jimmy Hinton	Clyde Morton
1960	Home Again Mike	PD	The Haberdasher	Ariel's Spunky Fireball	W. C. Jones	Paul Walker
1961	Spacemaster	PD	Fast Delivery	Knolwood Selene	Ralph E. Daniel	Paul Walker
1962	Home Again Hattie	PB	Home Again Mike	Hattie of Arkansas	V. E. Johnson	Jack Harper
1963	Stormy Tempest	PD	Stormy Mike	Anytime	Dr. W. G. Arney and S. W. Hart	Gene Lunsford
1964	War Storm	PD	Warhoop Jake	Satilla Little Jane	B. McCall	John S. Gates
1966	Safari	PB	Mercer Miller	Mercer Mill Judy	S. H. Vredenburgh	John Rex Gates
1967	Satilla Virginia Lady	PB	Satilla Midnight Sun	Lady Bess	Dr. F. M. Phillippi	Herman Smith
1968	Riggins White Knight	PD	Major Lexington Boy	Stanley's Candy	Dr. Nicholas E. Palumbo	D. Hoyle Eaton

Year	Winner		Sire	Dam		
1938	Uncas Flying Devil	PD	Haw Branch Spot	Beauty Uncas	Howard E. Eyster	W. D. English
1939	Amazon's Village Girl	PB	Village Boy	Spunky Creek Amazon	H. E. McGonigal	Howard Kirk
1940	Tarheelia's Lucky Strike	PD	Lexington Jake	Tarheelia's Best Bet	G. M. Livingston	Earl Crangle
1941	Rumson Farm Loch	SD	Equity	Queenie MacPherson	Ray Hoagland	G. M. Crangle
1942	Titan	PD	Spunky Creek Boy	Spunky Creek Joann	H. E. McGonigal	W. D. English
1943	Tarheelia's Lucky Strike	PD	Lexington Jake	Tarheelia's Best Bet	G. M. Livingston	G. M. Crangle
1944	Nomad White Boy*	PD	Even Money	Egyptian Willing Girl	C. G. Holt	W. L. Cosner
1945	Tyson	PD	Titan	Brenda Breeze	H. E. McGonigal	Howard Kirk
1946	Adonis Skyline Mike*	PD	Adonis	Melton's Dixie Lee	Dr. L. K. Firth	Jimmie Stewart
1947	Roger*	PD	Claussen's Ranger Doone	Homewood China Doll	Euclid Claussen	F. E. Bevan
1948	Shore's Brownie Doone	PD	Claussen's Ranger Doone	Devotion's Kate	G. M. Livingston	G. A. Evans Jr.
1949	Sam's Madison Jake*	PD	Sam's Maryland Jake	Lady Madison C	R. O. Carpenter	Lee Hoffman
1950	Kilsyth Brownie's Son	PD	Shore's Brownie Doone	Mary Karma	G. M. Livingston	G. A. Evans
1951	Kilsyth Rusty Doone*	PD	Shore's Brownie Doone	Aviette	Mrs. G. M. Livingston	G. A. Evans
1952	Kilsyth Rusty Doone	PD	Shore's Brownie Doone	Aviette	Mrs. G. M. Livingston	G. A. Evans
1953	Rumson Farm Hayride	PD	Louisiana Hayride	Nightcap's Aurora	Raymond Hoagland	Earl Crangle
1954	Kilsyth Georgia Rebel	PD	Shore's Brownie Doone	Kilsyth Delivery Dot	Mrs. G. M. Livingston	G. A. Evans
1955	Mitchina	PD	Accolade	Spunky's Jane Willing	H. W. Denham Jr.	Pete Smith
1956	Home Again Mike	PD	The Haberdasher	Ariel's Spunky Fireball	W. C. Jones	Paul Walker
1957	Rumson Farm Hayride	PD	Louisiana Hayride	Nightcap's Aurora	W. H. McNaughton	Earl Crangle
1958	Rumson Farm Hayride	PD	Louisiana Hayride	Nightcap's Aurora	Carmen Basilio and Earl Crangle	Earl Crangle
1959	Q's Delivery Doone	PD	Newman's Delivery Dan	McCall's Mary Doone	H. A. Crane	Earl Crangle
1960	Homerun Bess	PB	Homerun	Homerun Spinet	Claudia L. Phelps	Fred Arant
1961	Little Frenchman	PD	Devious	Sporty King	Peter Lusardi	Fred Arant
1962	Little Frenchman	PD	Devious	Sporty King	Peter Lusardi	P. A. Brousseau
1963	Rig A Jig	PD	Little Frenchman	Santee Tillie	A. L. Lippitt	P. A. Brousseau
1964	Rambling Rebel Dan	PD	Newman's Delivery Dan	Alicia's Image	W. S. Richardson	P. A. Brousseau
1965	Mike's Home Again	PD	Mike's Delivery	Rico Paladin's Belle	Dr. A. W. Simpson Jr.	Fred Arant Jr.
1966	Sugarshack	PB	War Storm	Sugarplum	Tom Peacock	Fred E. Bevan
1967	Tooth Acres Hawk	PD	Latham's White King	John Oliver's Susie	Dr. F. B. Hines Jr.	Bob Lamb
						Fred Arant Jr.

* Placed first—title withheld.

WINNERS OF THE NATIONAL FREE-FOR-ALL CHAMPIONSHIP

Year	Name	Breed and Sex	Sire	Dam	Owner	Handler
1916	John Proctor	PD	Fishel's Frank	Miss Mariutch	A. L. Curtis	C. H. Babcock
1917	De Soto Frank	PD	Fishel's Frank	Alford's John's Fancy	A. G. C. Sage	J. L. Holloway
1918	Candy Kid	SD	Vallejo	Bond's Gypsy	C. E. Duffield	Chesley H. Harris
1919	Jay R's Boy	SD	Jay R Whitestone	Trixie Danstone	Dr. T. H. Clark	Edw. Farrior
1920	Jay R's Boy	SD	Jay R Whitestone	Trixie Danstone	Dr. T. H. Clark	Edw. Farrior
1921	Shore's Ben	SD	Ben's Sport	Mollie Cummings	Dr. A. F. Stone	John W. Martin
1922	Becky Broom Hill	PB	Broom Hill Dan	Nell's Queen Cott	L. L. Haggin	Chesley H. Harris
1923	Muscle Shoals' Jake	PD	Ferris' Jake	Harris' Lady Pauper	James C. Foster Jr.	Edw. Farrior
1924	Muscle Shoals' Jake	PD	Ferris' Jake	Harris' Lady Pauper	James C. Foster Jr.	Mack Pritchette
1925	McTyre	PD	Milligan's Dan	McPherson's Choice	Jacob France	Chesley H. Harris
1926	Manrico	PD	Ferris' Jake	Griffith's Deenoya	C. E. Griffith	Pete Dixon
1927	McTyre	PD	Milligan's Dan	McPherson's Choice	Jacob France	Chesley H. Harris
1928	Ireland's Greymist	PB	Griffith's Jack	Burger's Johanna	H. Glenn Ireland	Mack Pritchette
1929	Superlette	PB	Milligan's Dan	Doughboy's Kelona Lady	A. G. C. Sage	Clyde Morton
1930	Mary Blue	PB	James Ben Hur	Lee's Grace	W. C. Teagle	Chesley H. Harris
1931	Superlette	PB	Milligan's Dan	Doughboy's Kelona Lady	A. G. C. Sage	Clyde Morton
1932	Superlette	PB	Milligan's Dan	Doughboy's Kelona Lady	A. G. C. Sage	Clyde Morton
1933	Norias Roy	PD	News Boy	Norias Lady	W. C. Teagle	Prather Robinson
1934	Spunky Creek Joann	PB	Muscle Shoals' Jake	Ireland's Greymist	Mrs. Nina Billingslea	Mack Pritchette
1935	Shanghai Express	PD	Richardson's Policeman	Touchstone Retrieving Roxy	G. M. Livingston	Henry Gilchrist
1936	Air Pilot's Sam	PD	Air Pilot	Nancy F	L. D. Johnson	Ed. Mack Farrior
1937	Timbuctoo	PD	The Hottentot	Lue's Sue	A. G. C. Sage	Ed. Mack Farrior
1938	Norias Aeroflow	PB	Norias Jeff	Norias Kate	W. C. Teagle	Chesley H. Harris
1939	Air Pilot's Sam	PD	Air Pilot	Nancy F	L. D. Johnson	Edw. Farrior
1940	Rockabye Baby	PB	Joe Willing	Lullaby	A. G. C. Sage	Clyde Morton
1941	The Texas Ranger	PD	Rex's Tarheel Jack	Miss Nellie Knolwood	D. B. McDaniel	Jack P. Harper
1942	Luminary	PD	Doctor Blue Willing	Lullaby	A. G. C. Sage	Clyde Morton
1943	The Texas Ranger	PD	Rex's Tarheel Jack	Miss Nellie Knolwood	D. B. McDaniel	Jack P. Harper
1944	Ariel	PD	Air Pilot's Sam	Lullaby	A. G. C. Sage	Clyde Morton
1945	Ariel	PD	Air Pilot's Sam	Lullaby	A. G. C. Sage	Clyde Morton

Year		Code				
1946	Saturn	PD	Luminary	Hostess	A. G. C. Sage	Clyde Morton
1947	Texan Boy	PD	The Texas Ranger	Nola II	D. B. McDaniel	Jack P. Harper
1948	Pandemonium	PD	Homerun Harrigan	Flying Girl	A. G. C. Sage	F. W. Frazier
1949	Pandemonium	PD	Homerun Harrigan	Flying Girl	A. G. C. Sage	F. W. Frazier
1950	Fast Delivery	PD	Delivery Boy	Ends Up	A. B. Bobbitt	Paul Walker
1951	Warhoop Jake	PD	Lester's Enjoy's Wahoo	Spunky Willing Diane	Dr. H. E. Longsdorf	Ed. Mack Farrior
1952	Warhoop Jake	PD	Lester's Enjoy's Wahoo	Spunky Willing Diane	Dr. H. E. Longsdorf	Ed. Mack Farrior
1953	Hall's Stonecroft Babe	PB	Tyson	Gold Flame	Mrs. A. A. Hall	Howard Kirk
1954	Lone Survivor	PD	Luminary	Titanette	Dr. E. R. Calame	Leon Covington
1955	Palamonium	PD	Paladin	Pandemonium's Dianah	James Hinton	Clyde Morton
1956	Volcano	PD	Tyson	Ranger's Ariel Girl	Marc F. Mitchell	Jack Harper
1957	Medallion	PD	Satilla Wahoo Pete	Sheila's Dot	S. H. Vredenburgh	John S. Gates
1958	Medallion	PD	Satilla Wahoo Pete	Sheila's Dot	S. H. Vredenburgh	John S. Gates
1959	Storm Trooper	PD	Stormy Mike	Bettie Shanks	B. McCall	John S. Gates
1960	Home Again Hattie	PB	Home Again Mike	Hattie of Arkansas	V. E. Johnson	Jack Harper
1961	Farmer's Secret Weapon	PD	Secret Weapon Boy	Farmer's Lady Tyson	Peter Lusardi	P. A. Brousseau
1962	Stormy Tempest	PD	Stormy Mike	Anytime	Dr. W. G. Arney and S. W. Hart	Gene Lunsford
1963	Canon	PD	Tradition	Stom's Judy	Jimmie Hinton	Jimmie Hinton
1964	War Storm	PD	Warhoop Jake	Satilla Little Jane	B. McCall	John S. Gates
1965	Paladin's Royal Flush	PD	Paladin's Royal Heir	Mike's Madonna	Rogers H. Hays	John Rex Gates
1966	Jorwick's Dixiecrat	PD	Storm's Romance	Neill Bickerstaff's Mary	G. Gunby Jordan	Winfred Campbell
1967	Riggins White Knight	PD	Major Lexington Boy	Stanley's Candy	R. W. Riggins	Dexter Hoyle Eaton
1968	Air Control	PD	Airflight	Sara Lee	W. W. Till	David Grubb

WINNERS OF THE GRAND NATIONAL GROUSE CHAMPIONSHIP

Year	Name	Breed and Sex	Sire	Dam	Owner	Handler
1943	Caviar	PD	Wautauga Joe	Gi Gi	C. R. Barton and J. A. Applegate	J. S. Applegate
1944	Hall's Black Rocket	SD	Sam L's Skyrocket	Gay Sandra	A. A. Hall	Gene Galloway
1945	No champion Declared					
1946	Burton's Fleetfoot Ginger	SD	Chester Valley Dick	Susie Beret	Mr. & Mrs. C. D. Burton	Roy Strickland
1947	The Texas Traveler	PD	The Texas Ranger	Dixieland Girl	Dr. A. L. Ziliak	Dr. A. L. Ziliak
1948	Title withheld					
1949	Sam L's Skyhigh	SD	Equity	Skyrocket's Starpoise	Sam R. Light	Larry Tuttle
1950	Sam L's Skyhigh	SD	Equity	Skyrocket's Starpoise	Sam R. Light	Larry Tuttle
1951	Trebor's Duchess	SB	Skyrocket's Flash Light	Conewango Lady	Leonard Sasso	W. A. Hugus
1952	Mistress Prettybones	PB	Garrison Hill Bombardier	Tick Thomee	Dr. J. H. Powers	Dr. J. H. Powers
1953	Puckety Village Boy	PD	Garrison Hill Bombardier	Triple Cities Whirlwind	E. D. McKean	Gene Galloway
1954	Tyson's Skyhills Flash	PD	Tyson	Ariel Spunky Girl	R. F. Papa	Carl Beattie
1955	Retina	SB	Retinoscope	Fiesta Flo	J. M. Hadaway	Luther Smith
1956	Retina	SB	Retinoscope	Fiesta Flo	R. L. Bruenner	Luther Smith
1957	Title withheld					
1958	Vigorous	PD	Frank's Boy Doc	Hunt's Lexington Judy	F. C. Ash	Luther Smith
1959	Doc's Girl Sis	PB	Frank's Boy Doc	Hunt's Lexington Judy	F. C. Ash	Luther Smith
1960	Sam L's Rebel	SD	Eugene Crockett II	Tenenssee Peerless Lou	Sam Light	Rich Tuttle
1961	Sam L's Rebel	SD	Eugene Crockett II	Tennessee Peerless Lou	Sam Light	Rich Tuttle
1962	Elhew Lucy Brown	PB	Elhew Zeus	Elhew Abbygail	R. C. Shear	Rich Tuttle

	Orchard Valley Melody	English SB	Orchard Valley Skylight	Fiesta Flo	R. P. Habgood Jr.	Luther Smith
1963						
1964	Title withheld	PB	Anna Monroe's Pete	Tyson's Gay Tune	A. Bartholomew	A. Bartholomew
1965	Brenda Wahoo	SB	Skyhigh's Buckey	Marshall's Gold Dust	K. E. Undercoffer	A. I. Undercoffer
1966	Hussy	PB	Elhew Speculator	Elhew Grouse Queen	R. C. Shear & R. G. Wehle	R. C. Shear
1967	Elhew Holly					

*Title withheld — placed first.